The Book You Wish Your Parents Had Read (and Your Children Will be Glad That You Did)

PHILIPPA PERRY

PENGUIN LIFE

AN IMPRINT OF

PENGUIN BOOK

KU-001-537

This book is dedicated with love to my sister Belinda

PENGUIN LIFE

UK | USA | Canada | Ireland | Australia
India | New Zealand | South Africa

Penguin Life is part of the Penguin Random House group of companies
whose addresses can be found at global.penguinrandomhouse.com.

Penguin
Random House
UK

First published 2019
This edition published with new material 2020
001

Copyright © Philippa Perry, 2019, 2020

The moral right of the author has been asserted

Set in 11/13 pt Dante MT Std
Typeset by Jouve (UK), Milton Keynes
Printed and bound in Great Britain by Clays Ltd, Elcograf S.p.A.

The authorized representative in the EEA is Penguin Random House Ireland,
Morrison Chambers, 32 Nassau Street, Dublin D02 YH68

A CIP catalogue record for this book is available from the British Library

ISBN: 978-0-241-25102-7

www.greenpenguin.co.uk

Contents

Contents

Foreword

This is not a straightforward parenting book.

I'm not going to go into details about potty-training or weaning.

This book is about how we have relationships with our children, what gets in the way of a good connection and what can enhance it.

It's about how we were brought up and how that has a bearing on how we parent, about the mistakes we'll make – especially those we never wanted to make – and what to do about them.

You will not find many tips, tricks or parenting hacks in this book, and at times it may upset you, make you angry or even make you a better parent.

I wrote the book I wish I had read as a new parent, and I really wish my parents had read it.

Introduction

Recently, I watched a stand-up routine by the comedian Michael McIntyre in which he said there are four things we need to do with our children: get them dressed, feed them, wash them and put them to bed. He said before he had his children he had a fantasy that being a parent would be all running through meadows and eating picnics, but the reality was that each day was an ongoing battle getting them to do just these four basic things. There was much laughter from the audience as he described persuading them to have their hair washed, to put on a coat, to go outside or to eat a vegetable. It was the laughter of parents, maybe parents like us, who've been there too. Being a parent* can be hard work. It can be boring, dispiriting, frustrating and taxing while at the same time being the funniest, most joyful, most love-filled, brilliant thing you'll ever experience.

When you're bogged down in the minutiae of nappies, childhood illnesses, tantrums (toddler and teenage), or when you're doing a full day's work and coming home to your real work, which includes scraping banana out of cracks in the high chair, or another letter from the headteacher summoning you to the school, it can be hard to put being a parent in perspective. This book is about giving you that big picture, to help you pull back,

---

* When I use the word 'parent' I mean someone who is responsible for children belonging to them, whether biologically, legally or as a close relative or friend; in other words, 'parent' could be interchangeable with 'primary caregiver'. Sometimes I use the word 'carer'; this can mean parent, surrogate parent, step-parent, paid or unpaid help or anyone who has principle responsibility for the child.

to see what matters and what doesn't, and what you can do to help your child be the person they can be.

The core of parenting is the relationship you have with your child. If people were plants, the relationship would be the soil. The relationship supports, nurtures, allows growth – or inhibits it. Without a relationship they can lean on, a child's sense of their security is compromised. You want the relationship to be a source of strength for your child – and, one day, for their children too.

As a psychotherapist, I've had the experience of listening to and talking to people who struggle with different aspects of parenting. Through my work I have had the opportunity to look at how relationships become dysfunctional – and what makes them work well again. The objective of this book is to share with you what is relevant when it comes to parenting. This will include how to work with feelings – yours and theirs – how to attune yourself to your children so you can learn to understand them better and how to have a real connection with them rather than getting stuck in exhausting patterns of conflict or withdrawal.

I take the long-term view on parenting rather than a tips-and-tricks approach. I am interested in how we can relate to our children rather than how we can manipulate them. In this book I encourage you to look at your own babyhood and childhood experiences so that you can pass on the good that was done to you by your own upbringing and hold back on the less helpful aspects of it. I'll be looking at how we can make all our relationships better and good for our children to grow up among. I'll cover how our attitudes in pregnancy can have a bearing on our future bond with our child, and how to be with a baby, a child, an adolescent or an adult child so you can have a relationship with them that is a source of strength to them and satisfaction to you. And, along the way, have far fewer battles about getting them dressed, fed, washed and put to bed.

This book is for parents who not only love their children but want to like them too.

PART ONE

Your Parenting Legacy

The cliché is true: children do not do what we say; they do what we do. Before we even consider the behaviour of our children, it's useful – essential, even – to look at their first role models. And one of them is you.

This section is all about you, because you will be a major influence on your child. In it, I'll give examples of how the past can affect the present when it comes to your relationship with your child. I will talk about how a child can often trigger old feelings in us that we then mistakenly act on in our dealings with them. I'll also be looking at the importance of examining our own inner critic so we do not pass too much of its damaging effects on to the next generation.

The past comes back to bite us (and our children)

A child needs warmth and acceptance, physical touch, your physical presence, love plus boundaries, understanding, play with people of all ages, soothing experiences and a lot of your attention and your time. Oh, so that's simple then: the book can end here. Except it can't, because things get in the way. Your life can get in the way: circumstances, childcare, money, school, work, lack of time and busyness . . . and this is not an exhaustive list, as you know.

But what can get in the way more than any of this, however, is what was given to us when we ourselves were babies and children. If we don't look at how we were brought up and the legacy of that, it can come back to bite us. You might have found yourself saying something along the lines of: 'I opened my mouth and my mother's words came out.' Of course, if theirs were words that made you feel wanted, loved and safe as a child, that would be fine. But so often they are the words that did the opposite.

What can get in the way are things like our own lack of confidence, our pessimism, our defences, which block our feelings, and our fear of being overwhelmed by feelings. Or when it comes specifically to relating to our children, it could be what irritates us about them, our expectations for them, or our fears for them. We are but a link in a chain stretching back through millennia and forward until who knows when.

The good news is you can learn to reshape your link, and this will improve the life of your children and their children, and you can start now. You don't have to do everything that was done to you; you can ditch the things that were unhelpful. If you are a parent or are going to be one, you can unpack and become familiar with your childhood, examine what happened to you, how you felt about it then, how you feel about it now, and, after having done that unpacking and taken a good look at it all, put back only what you need.

If, when you were growing up, you were, for the most part, respected as a unique and valuable individual, shown unconditional love, given enough positive attention and had rewarding relationships with your family members, you will have received a blueprint to create positive, functional relationships. In turn, this would have shown you that you could positively contribute to your family and to your community. If all this is true of you, then the exercise of examining your childhood is unlikely to be too painful.

If you did not have a childhood like this – and that's the case for a large proportion of us – looking back on it may bring emotional discomfort. I think it is necessary to become more self-aware around that discomfort so that we can become more mindful of ways to stop us passing it on. So much of what we have inherited sits just outside of our awareness. That makes it hard sometimes to know whether we are reacting in the here and now to our child's behaviour or whether our responses are more rooted in our past.

I think this story will help to illustrate what I mean. It was told to me by Tay, a loving mum and senior psychotherapist who trains other psychotherapists. I'm mentioning both her roles to make it clear that even the most self-aware and well-meaning of us can slip into an emotional time warp and find ourselves reacting to our past rather than to what's happening here in the present. This story begins when Tay's daughter Emily, who was nearly seven, shouted to her that she was stuck on a climbing frame, that she needed help to get off.

I told her to get down and, when she said she couldn't, I suddenly felt furious. I thought she was being ridiculous – she could easily get down herself. I shouted, 'Get down this minute!'

She eventually did. Then she tried to hold my hand, but I was still furious, and I said no, and then she howled.

Once we got home and made tea together she calmed down and I wrote off the whole thing to myself as 'God, kids can be a pain.'

Fast-forward a week: we're at the zoo and there's another climbing frame. Looking at it, I felt a flash of guilt. It obviously reminded Emily of the previous week too, because she looked up at me almost fearfully.

I asked her if she wanted to play on it. This time, instead of sitting on a bench looking at my phone, I stood by the frame and watched her. When she felt she'd got stuck, she held out her arms to me for help. But this time I was more encouraging. I said, 'Put one foot there and the other there and grab that and you'll be able to do it by yourself.' And she did.

When she had got down, she said, 'Why didn't you help me last time?'

I thought about it, and I said, 'When I was little, Nana treated me like a princess and carried me everywhere, told me to "be careful" all the time. It made me feel incapable of doing anything for myself and I ended up with no confidence. I don't want that to happen to you, which is why I didn't want to help when you asked to be lifted off the climbing frame last week. And it reminded me of being your age, when I wasn't allowed to get down by myself. I was overcome with anger and I took it out on you, and that wasn't fair.'

Emily looked up at me and said, 'Oh, I just thought you didn't care.'

'Oh no,' I said. 'I care, but at that moment I didn't know that I was angry at Nana and not at you. And I'm sorry.'

Like Tay, it's easy to fall into making instant judgements or assumptions about our emotional reaction without considering that it may be as much to do with what's being triggered in our own background as with what's happening now.

But when you feel anger – or any other difficult emotions, including resentment, frustration, envy, disgust, panic, irritation, dread, fear, et cetera – in response to something your child has done or requested, it's a good idea to think of it as a warning. Not a warning that your child or children are necessarily doing anything wrong but that your own buttons are being pressed.

Often the pattern works like this: when you react with anger or another overly charged emotion around your child it is because it's a way you have learned to defend yourself from feeling what you felt at their age. Outside of your awareness, their behaviour is threatening to trigger your own past feelings of despair, of longing, of loneliness, jealousy or neediness. And so you unknowingly take the easier option: rather than empathizing with what your child is feeling, you short-circuit to being angry or frustrated or panicked.

Sometimes the feelings from the past that are being re-triggered go back more than one generation. My mother used to find the shrieks of children at play irritating. I noticed that I too went into a sort of alert state when my own child and her friends were making a noise, even though they were enjoying themselves appropriately. I wanted to find out more, so I asked my mother what would have happened to her if she had played noisily as a child. She told me her father – my grandfather – had been over fifty when she was born, he often had bad headaches and all the children had to tiptoe around the house or they got into trouble.

Maybe you're scared if you admit that, at times, your irritation with your child gets the upper hand, thinking it will intensify those angry feelings or somehow make them more real. But, in fact, naming our inconvenient feelings to ourselves and finding an alternative narrative for them – one where we don't hold our children responsible – means we won't judge our children as being somehow at fault for having triggered them. If you can do this, it makes you less likely to act out on that feeling at the expense of your child. You will not always be able to trace a story that makes sense of how you feel, but that doesn't mean there isn't one, and it can be helpful to hold on to that.

One issue might be that as a child you felt that the people who loved you perhaps didn't always like you. They might sometimes have found you annoying, hard work, disappointing, unimportant, exasperating, clumsy or stupid. When you're reminded of this by your own child's behaviour, you are triggered and you end up shouting or acting out whatever your default negative behaviour is.

There's no doubt it can feel hard, becoming a parent. Overnight, your child becomes your most demanding priority, 24/7. Having a child may have even made you finally realize what your own parents had to deal with, maybe to appreciate them more, to identify with them more or to feel more compassion for them. But you need to identify with your own child or children too. Time spent contemplating what it may have felt like for you as a baby or a child around the same age as your own child will help you develop empathy for your child. That will help you understand and feel with them when they behave in a way that triggers you into wanting to push them away.

I had a client, Oskar, who had adopted a little boy of eighteen months old. Every time his son dropped food on the floor, or left his food, Oskar felt rage rise up in him. I asked him what would have happened to him as a child if he'd dropped or left food? He remembered his grandfather rapping his knuckles with the handle of a knife then making him leave the room. After he got back in touch with what it had felt like for him as a little boy when he was treated like that, he found compassion for his own self as a toddler, which in turn helped him find patience for his child.

It's easy to assume our feelings belong with what's happening in front of us and are not simply a reaction to what happened in the past. As an example, imagine you have a four-year-old child who gets a huge pile of presents on their birthday and you sharply call them 'spoilt' for not sharing one of their new toys.

What is happening here? Logically, it's not their fault if they are the recipient of so much stuff. You may unconsciously be assuming they are undeserving of so many things and your irritation at that leaks out in a sharp tone or by you unreasonably expecting them to be more mature.

If you stop to look back, to become interested in your irritation towards them, what you might find is that your own inner four-year-old is jealous or feels competitive. Maybe at the age of four you were told to share something you didn't want to share, or you simply weren't given many things and, in order not to feel sad for four-year-old you, you lash out at your child.

I'm reminded of the hate mail and negative social media attention anyone in the public eye receives from anonymous sources. If you read between the lines, what it seems to be saying more than anything is, *It's not fair that you're famous and I'm not.* It's not so unusual to feel jealous of our children. If you do, you need to own it, not act out negatively towards your child because of it. They don't need parental trolling.

Throughout this book I have put in exercises that may help you have a deeper understanding of what I'm talking about. If you find them unhelpful or overwhelming, you can skip them, and perhaps come back to them when you feel more ready.

Exercise: Where does this emotion come from?

The next time you feel anger towards your child (or any other overly charged emotion), rather than unthinkingly responding, stop to ask yourself: Does this feeling wholly belong to this situation and my child in the present? How am I stopping myself seeing the situation from their standpoint?

One good way to stop yourself from reacting is to say, 'I need some time to think about what's happening,' and to use that time to calm down. Even if your child does need some guidance, there's not much point in doing it when you're angry. If you give it then, they will hear only your anger and not what you are trying to tell them.

You can do this second variation of the exercise even if you do not yet have a child. Just notice how often you feel angry, or self-righteous, or indignant, or panicky or perhaps ashamed, or self-loathing or disconnected. Look for patterns in your responses. Look back to when you first felt this feeling, tracing it back to your childhood, where you began to respond like this, and you may begin to understand to what extent this reaction has become a habit. In other words, the response is at least as much due to it having become a habit in you than it is to do with the situation in the present.

Rupture and repair

In an ideal world, we would catch ourselves before we ever acted out on a feeling inappropriately. We would never shout at our child or threaten them or make them feel bad about themselves in any way. Of course, it's unrealistic to think we would be able to do this every time. Look at Tay – she's an experienced psychotherapist and she still acted on her fury because she thought it belonged to the present. But one thing she did do, and what we can all learn to do, to mend the hurt is called 'rupture and repair'. Ruptures – those times when we misunderstand each other, where we make wrong assumptions, where we hurt someone – are inevitable in every important, intimate and familial relationship. It is not the rupture that is so important, it is the repair that matters.

The way to make repairs in relationships is firstly by working to change your responses, that is, to recognize your triggers and use that knowledge to react in a different way. Or, if your child is old enough to understand, you can use words and apologize, as Tay did to Emily. Even if you only realize that you acted wrongly towards your child many moons after it happened, you can still tell them where you got it wrong. It can mean a tremendous amount to a child, even an adult child, when a parent makes a repair. Look at the belief that Emily was carrying. She assumed Tay, on some level, did not care about her. What a relief to learn her mother did care and had merely been in a muddle.

A parent once asked me whether it was dangerous to apologize to children. 'But don't they need you to be right, otherwise they won't feel secure?' she asked. No! What children need is for us to be real and authentic, not perfect.

Think back to your childhood: were you made to feel 'bad' or in the wrong, or even responsible for your parents' bad moods? If it happened to you, it is all too easy to try to repair your feeling of being wrong by making someone else feel wrong, and the victims of this are, far too often, our children.

A child's own instincts will tell them when we are not in tune with them or with what's happening and, if we pretend that we are, we will dull their instincts. For example, if we pretend that, as adults, we are never wrong, the result can be a child who overadapts – not only to what you say, but to what anyone may say. Then they can become more vulnerable to people who may not have their best interests at heart. Instinct is a major component in confidence, competence and intelligence, so it's a good idea not to damage or warp your child's.

I met Mark when he came to a parenting workshop I was running – his wife, Toni, had suggested he attend. At the time, their son, Toby, was nearly two. Mark told me he and his wife had agreed not to have children but that, at the age of forty, Toni changed her mind. After a year of trying and a year of IVF, she got pregnant.

> Considering we worked so hard in getting there, it surprises me now, looking back, how hazy I was about what life with a baby would be like. I think I must've got my idea of parenthood from watching television, when the baby is miraculously mostly asleep in a cot and hardly ever cries.
>
> Once Toby was born, the reality of no longer having any spontaneity and flexibility, of the tedium of a baby, of one of us always being on baby duty around the clock, meant I began to swing between feeling resentful or depressed or both.
>
> Two years on, I'm still not enjoying my life. Toni and I don't talk about anything other than Toby and, if I try to talk about something else, it reverts to him in under a minute. I know I'm being selfish but that doesn't stop me feeling like I'm on a short fuse. I don't see myself living with Toni and Toby for much longer, to be honest.

I asked Mark to tell me about his childhood. All he could say was that he wasn't very interested in exploring it with me, as it had been completely normal. As a psychotherapist, I took 'not being interested' as a clue he wanted to distance himself from it. I suspected that being a parent was triggering feelings in him that he wanted to run away from.

19

I asked Mark what 'normal' meant. He told me his dad left when he was three and, as he grew up, his father's visits became less and less frequent. Mark is right: this is a normal childhood. However, that does not mean that the disappearance of his father didn't matter to him.

I asked Mark how he'd felt about his father's desertion, and he couldn't remember. I suggested it was perhaps too painful to remember. And perhaps it felt easier to be like his own dad and to leave Toni and Toby because then he didn't have to unlock his own box of difficult emotions. I told him I thought it was important that he did indeed unlock and open it because, otherwise, he wouldn't be sensitive to the needs of his own son and would pass down to Toby what had been passed down to him. I wasn't sure from his response if he heard what I was actually saying.

I didn't see Mark until six months later, at a different workshop. He told me he'd been feeling depressed and, rather than just dismissing it, he'd decided to start having therapy. To his surprise, he told me, he found himself crying and shouting in the therapist's room about his own father leaving him.

Therapy helped me put the feelings where they needed to be – with the desertion of my dad, rather than thinking I just wasn't cut out to be in this relationship or to be a parent.

I'm not saying I don't still feel bored, or even resentful sometimes, but I know that resentment belongs in my past. I know it's not about Toby.

I can see the point of all the attention I give to Toby now; it's to make him feel good, not just now but in the future. Toni and I are filling him up with love and, hopefully, that will mean he has love to give when he's older, so he will feel valuable. I have no relationship with my own father. I know Toby is getting from me what I didn't get from my own dad, that we are laying the foundations of a great relationship.

> Seeing the point of what I'm doing has turned most of my discontent to hope and gratitude. I feel closer to Toni again now too. Now I am more interested in and present with Toby, it has freed Toni up to think of other things apart from him.

Mark repaired the rupture with Toby – his desire to desert him – by looking into his own past in order to understand what was happening in the present. Then he was able to change his attitude towards being with his son. It was as though he could not unlock his love until he had unlocked his grief.

Repairing the past

Some time ago, a mother-to-be asked me what my one suggestion for a new parent would be. I told her, whatever age your child is, they are liable to remind you, on a bodily level, of the emotions you went through when you were at a similar stage. She looked at me, a bit bemused.

A year or so later, with a toddler at her feet, that same mum told me that she hadn't understood what I meant at the time. But she'd remembered it and, as she grew into her new role, it had begun to make so much sense and had helped her to feel for her child as well. You won't remember consciously what it's like to be a baby, but on other levels you will remember, and your child will keep reminding you.

It is common for a parent to withdraw from their child at a very similar age to when that parent's parent became unavailable to them. Or a parent will want to pull away emotionally when their child is the same age as they were when they felt alone. Mark is a classic example of someone who didn't want to face up to the feelings his child was bringing up in him.

You might want to run away from these feelings, and from

your child too, but if you do you will pass down what was done to you. There will be plenty of good stuff you will be passing on too – all that love you received – but what you don't want to pass on is your inherited fear, hate, loneliness or resentment. There will be times when you feel unpleasant emotions towards or around your child, just like you occasionally may towards your partner, your parent, your friend or yourself. If you admit this, then you will be less likely to be unthinkingly punishing them for whatever feeling they have brought up in you.

If you find, as Mark did, that you resent family life because you feel pushed aside, it could be because you were pushed aside as a child and not considered in one or both of your parents' lives. Sometimes this resentment can feel more like boredom or a feeling of disconnection from your child.

Some parents think I'm exaggerating when I use words like 'desertion' and 'resentment'. 'I don't resent my children,' they say. 'Sometimes I want to be left alone in peace, but I love them.' I think of desertion as a spectrum. On the most severe end, there's the actual desertion of physically removing yourself from the child's life entirely, like Mark's father did. But I also consider desertion to include pushing a child away when they want your attention or not really listening to them when they are trying to, for example, show you their painting (which is your child trying to show you, on one level, who they really are).

This feeling of wanting to push children away, of wanting them to sleep long and to play independently before they are ready so they don't take up your time, can come about when you're trying not to feel with your child because they're such a painful reminder of your childhood. Because of this, you're un-able to surrender to their needs. It's true we may tell ourselves we push our children away because we want more of the other areas of our lives, such as work, friends and Netflix, but we are the grown-ups here. We know that this needy stage is just that, a stage, whereas our work, friends and other leisure pursuits can be picked up when this small person does not need us so much.

It is hard to face up to this, to stop how we ourselves were treated being passed on to another generation. We need to notice how we feel, then reflect on that, rather than react to any feelings we don't properly understand. Facing up to the less acceptable ways we might want to act – in Mark's case, for example, running away – can also bring up feelings of shame. When this happens there's a tendency to get defensive so as not to feel the shame. And if we do that, we change nothing and we pass our dysfunction on to another generation. But shame doesn't kill us. When we realize what is happening, we can turn our shame into pride because we noticed how we felt compelled to act and became aware of how we needed to change.

What really matters is being comfortable with your child, making them feel safe and that you want to be around them. The words we use are a small part of that; a bigger part is our warmth, our touch, our goodwill and the respect we show them: respect for their feelings, their person, their opinions and their interpretation of their world. In other words, we need to show the love we feel for them when they are awake, not just when they look beautiful asleep.

If you feel yourself wanting a break from your children every hour of every day, what you probably need is a break from the feelings they trigger in you. To avoid being controlled by those triggers, look back at yourself as a baby or as a child with compassion. Once you've been able to do that, you will be able to identify with the need and longing your children have for you. It is of course important to get a babysitter from time to time and to enjoy some adult pursuit, but be aware if the feeling of wanting a break feels particularly charged and seems to be there most of the time, then dare to remember what it felt like when you were the same age as your child is now.

Exercise: Looking back with compassion

Ask yourself what behaviour in your child triggers the strongest negative response in you. What happened to you as a child when you demonstrated the same behaviour?

Exercise: Message from your memories

Close your eyes and remember your very earliest memory. It may just be an image or a feeling, or it may have a story. What is the predominant emotion in your memory? What relevance can you trace from the memory to who you are now? How does the memory influence how you parent? Remember: if anything comes up when you do this exercise, for example a fear of feeling ashamed, which may now be causing you always rigidly to cling on to being right, perhaps at the expense of your child, feel proud of yourself for having spotted it rather than feeling like you will collapse under the shame or defensively steering away and carrying on with the behaviour you enact in response to that feeling.

How we talk to ourselves

As I said at the start of this section, children do what we do rather than what we say. So, if you are in the habit of beating yourself up in your head, your child is liable to adopt the same potentially damaging habit.

One of my earliest memories is my mother looking in the mirror and picking fault with herself. And when, years later, I did the exact same thing in front of my astute teenage daughter, she told me she didn't like it when I did this, and I listened and remembered how I hadn't liked it either.

Our inherited patterns of being and behaving can often be found in how we talk to ourselves, especially via our inner faultfinder. Almost all of us have in our heads a sort of continual chatter or commentary that we are so used to we don't really notice what it's saying. But this voice can be a harsh inner critic. Maybe you tell yourself stuff like 'That's not for the likes of me', or it could be 'You can't trust anyone', 'I'm hopeless', 'I'm never good enough, I should just give up', 'I can't do anything right', 'I'm too fat' or 'I'm useless.' Be careful of such inner talk because not only will it have a powerful steer on your own life but it will also have an impact on your child's life, influencing them to judge themselves and others.

Apart from teaching your child to make harmful judgements, that inner negative voice finds ways to exaggerate a low mood, knock confidence and make us feel generally inadequate. And there's another good reason for you to catch how you talk to yourself: it seems that we pass on our inner voices to our children (as well as our habits in plain sight). If you want your children to have the capacity for happiness, the thing that may get in the way more than many others is your self-critic.

We are formed into adults by our childhood experiences – it's the fundamental way in which we humans develop – but it is hard to shake off. It can be difficult to stop this inner critical voice, but what you can do is notice when you are doing it and give yourself a pat on the back for noticing.

Elaine is the mother of two children and works as an art-gallery assistant. She is aware of her inner negative voice:

> It's usually about failure. That I shouldn't try something because it won't work . . . I'll be bad at it . . . I'll embarrass myself. So I dissuade myself from doing things. Then I criticize myself for being unadventurous and not applying myself. I tell myself I don't stick at things, that I'm shallow and have no real passion for or expertise in anything. Just saying this to you now, I can hear the voice in my head saying, 'Yeah, well, all those things are true.'
>
> I feel guilty when I think about who this voice may have come from, because I love my mum very much. I have always

known she loves me, always felt very loved. But Mum is a worrier, has never felt good enough, has a lot of negativity. She is, and always has been, hard on herself. She can never take a compliment. To 'What a delicious lasagne!', she'll reply, 'No flavour and too much cheese.'

Somehow, she passed on this not-good-enough vibe to my sisters and me. We dwell on our failures and use them as evidence that we're no good and shouldn't even bother. Once, I got a B in French and it felt like the end of the world.

Mum does try to be positive, but it'll be undermined with an unguarded comment. At the final fitting for my wedding dress I came out of the changing room and Mum pursed her lips, looked worried, and said, 'Yes, yes, on the day, with the flowers and veil and everything, that'll do.' Unwittingly, her own anxiety and insecurities can lay waste to the people around her.

As well as having a self-torturous inner critic, Elaine said her mother also got a lot right – and I in no way want to demonize her – but, like most of us, it seems she may have been unaware of how she talked to herself, and especially how her inner critic could be passed on to her children.

When you notice how you talk to yourself, it gives you more choice about how you listen to that voice. This is how Elaine has learned to deal with her inner critic:

I'm determined not to pass it on to my children. I do not want them to have my fear of failing. It's so demoralizing.

I used to argue with what the voice said, and I always lost (plus, this used up so much energy and attention). Recently, I've found the best way is to not engage with the voice. I almost treat it as I would a difficult work colleague, tell it, 'Well, you're entitled to your opinion.'

I try to do the things the inner critic tells me I can't do. I make myself override my fears in order not to discourage my kids, to show them it's not so bad to fail. I have taken up painting again, despite the voice telling me to give up. Rather than judging what I paint, I am training myself to notice what I enjoy about it and which bits of each painting please me. An unexpected side effect of this has been more confidence, not only about my painting but about life in general.

If we separate the content of what Elaine is doing into a process, it goes like this:

1. First, recognize the voice.
2. Don't engage with it or argue with it. Instead, treat it like somebody awkward who you can shake off if you acknowledge what they've said but without colluding with them, by thinking, for example, 'You are entitled to your opinion.'
3. Expand your comfort zone. By doing the thing your inner critic says you can't, you'll find more confidence. It's a real thing you can remember when self-doubt creeps in.
4. Being aware of the dangers of passing your inner critic on to your child will give you an extra incentive to be mindful of it.

Exercise: Reveal your inner critic

Keep a pencil and pad to hand and note down any self-critical thoughts you have throughout the day. Do you recognize these criticisms as ones you have seen others articulate in your past?

Think of something you would like to achieve and the steps you would need to take to get there. Now notice how you talk to yourself about this thing. Are you saying anything to stop yourself? Does this voice remind you of anyone else?

Good parent/bad parent: the downside of judgement

The very fact you're reading this means you want to be the best parent you can. One thing that stops this is judgement, both of yourself and of other people. How we judge ourselves as parents is my bugbear.

'Good parent/bad parent' labels are not helpful because they are about extremes. It's impossible to be perfectly attuned to our children all the time, and even some good intentions can have harmful consequences. But because nobody wants to be labelled a 'bad parent', when we make mistakes (and we all do), wanting to avoid the label makes us pretend we haven't made them.

Partly due to these labels of 'good mother', 'bad dad', or vice versa, existing, to avoid the humiliation of being in the bad role, we get defensive about anything we may be doing wrong. That means we do not examine or look at the ways we are misattuning to our children or neglecting their emotional needs. We don't look how to improve our relationships with them. It may also mean we hide from ourselves the things we may be doing wrong behind the things we do right, so we can cling to the identity of 'good' mother or father.

Parental fear of facing up to where we might be going wrong doesn't help our children either. Mistakes – pretending our child's feelings don't matter, or whatever else we've done wrong – matter so much less when we change our behaviour and repair any rupture. But we cannot put anything right if it feels too shaming to admit our faults – and this label of 'bad' adds to that shame.

Let's drop 'good' and 'bad' as attributes for mothers and fathers. No one is wholly saint or sinner. A grumpy, honest parent (normally written off as 'bad') may be a better parent than a frustrated and resentful parent hiding behind a façade of syrupy sweetness. I'd go further. Just as we shouldn't judge ourselves, we should try not to judge our children. It is satisfying to put something in a box, label it and forget about it, but it is not good for us and it certainly isn't good for the person in the box. It's not helpful to judge a child as bad or good, or indeed to judge them as anything, because it's hard to thrive with the restriction of a label: 'the quiet one', 'the clumsy one', 'the noisy one' . . .

Human beings change and grow all the time, especially small ones. It is far better to describe what you see and say what you appreciate rather than judge. So say, 'I liked how hard you were concentrating when you did those sums' rather than 'You're great at maths.' Say, 'I am impressed how much thought you have put into this drawing. I like how the house looks like it's smiling. It makes me feel happy.' Not 'Lovely picture.' Praise effort, describe what you see and feel and encourage your child without judging. Describing and finding something specific to appreciate is far more encouraging than a non-specific judgement of 'Great job' and far, far more useful than criticism. If a whole page of writing is nearly a completely untidy mess but the letter P is perfectly formed, all you need to say is, 'I like how neatly you've written that P.' Hopefully, next time, you'll like another letter as well.

Exercise: No more judging

Instead of judging yourself on what you make and do, observe and appreciate what you get right instead. Notice the difference in how it makes you feel. For example, rather than saying or thinking something like, 'I make great bread,' try 'Concentrating on my baking is paying off.' Rather than 'I'm bad at yoga,' try instead 'I have made a start at yoga and I've improved since last week.' It's not so much the words – I'm not totally banning 'good' or 'bad' – it's about suspending judgement or holding our conclusions lightly rather than rigidly. This will do less harm to ourselves and to our children.

I have started this book by looking at you rather than concentrating on your child because what makes a child the unique individual they are (or will be, if they are not yet with us) is a matchless mix of genes and environment, and you are a major part of your child's environment.

How we feel about ourselves and how much responsibility we take for how we react to our children are key aspects of parenting that are too often overlooked because it's much easier to focus instead on our children and their behaviours rather than examining how they affect us and then how we in turn affect them. And it is not only how we respond to children that shapes their personality traits and character but also what they witness and feel in their environment.

I hope I've convinced you to examine how you react to the feelings your children trigger in you. Be aware of how you talk to yourself. Look out for your inner critic. And be less judgemental – about yourself, your parenting and your children.

PART TWO

Your Child's Environment

A counsellor recently told me a story about working with a refugee family. He was trying to empathize with them and to understand what it must be like to have no permanent home. One of the children piped up, 'Oh, we've got a home, we've just got nowhere to put it yet.'

I was moved when I heard this remark. It sums up how the love and care between family members can be a safety net, which is something we all need. So, how can we take steps to ensure the relationships that make up being a family feel like a sanctuary? This is what I will be looking at in this section: how to build a family environment where your children will thrive.

It's not family structure that matters, it's how we all get on

You and whoever you live with is your children's environment. A large part of how your children go on to feel about themselves and how they interact with others will form in relationship to you and the small circle around you. That's your co-parent, if you have one, siblings, grandparents, paid help and close friends.

It is important to have awareness about how we behave in these relationships. For example, do we bring our appreciation to the people close to us or do we dump our anger on to them? These familial relationships are influential in determining how a child's personality and mental health develop. Children are individuals, but they are part of a whole system too. As well as close family relationships, a child's system also includes school, their own friendships and the wider culture. It makes sense to look at that system and do what you can to make it the best possible environment for you and for your child. It doesn't have to be perfect – perfect doesn't exist.

It's not the structure of the family that matters, which is good news if you're not in a nuclear family. The arrangements can be as conventional or as unconventional as you like; parents can live apart, or together, in a commune or a *ménage à trois*, they can be gay, straight or bisexual – it doesn't matter. Research has shown that family structure itself has little effect on children's cognitive or emotional development and, in fact, over 25 per cent of children are brought up in single-parent families in the UK, with around half of these single parents having been in a partnership at the time of the birth of their child, and they do no better or worse than children from a more conventional set-up, once factors such as their financial situation and parental education are taken into consideration.

The people in a child's life comprise that child's world. It can be one of richness and love but it can also be a battleground. It matters more than most adults think that family life does not veer too far towards the battleground end of the scale. If children are preoccupied, if they are worried about their security, their safety and how they belong, they are not free to be curious about the wider world. Not being curious impacts negatively upon how they concentrate and learn.

In one survey, teenagers and parents were asked whether they agreed or disagreed with the following statement: 'Parents getting on well is one of the most important factors in raising happy children.' Seventy per cent of teenagers agreed compared to only 33 per cent of parents.

This could be because the emotional distress children go through when their parents' and carers' relationships aren't functional isn't visible to the grown-ups. You may know how hard it is for you, as a parent, to look at your child's pain. And, therefore, it's really hard to look at how your own actions may have contributed to that pain.

You may feel justified in acting the way you do, or helpless at the idea of changing your behaviour. It may feel daunting or even overwhelming for you to look at how you interact with your co-parent and other close members of your family, but I hope in this part of the book I can give you some ideas on how to make improvements if you need to.

When parents aren't together

Even if you live apart from your child's other parent, what matters is that you refer to them in respectful ways, that you can appreciate their good points and not always be emphasizing their faults. I know this may seem impossible to some people, especially after a difficult break-up. It may make it easier for you when I tell you how important it is for a child: they see themselves as belonging, attached to and part of each of you. If one half of the partnership that brought them into being is often referred to as somehow being a 'bad' person, that is all too often internalized by the child so that they too see themselves as a 'bad' person. A child can also be torn apart by the pull to be loyal to both their parents.

So what's the best way to negotiate a split? A child fares better afterwards if the parents cooperate with each other and communicate well and if the child continues to have regular close contact with both parents. If you can manage that, your child is less likely to become depressed or aggressive. As for the child's relationship with their non-resident parent, this also works better if there is clear, positive communication between the parents. If one parent (it is often the father, but not always) drifts away after separation, the child is more likely to suffer distress, anger, depression or low self-esteem. That's why it's such a worry that, in the UK, more than a quarter of children whose parents have split up have no further contact with their father three years after the event.

I understand it is not always possible to get along with an ex, as this story I'm about to share shows. Mel is mum to a six-year-old son, Noah. She had a relationship with Noah's father, James, for five years. They often lived in different countries and didn't see themselves as a committed couple, but they enjoyed each other's company hugely when they did get together. Mel's story may sound extreme, but anyone who's had parenting disagreements with an ex may find it useful.

When Mel got pregnant, James assumed she would have an abortion. When she didn't, he was furious and tried to sever their connection. Now, he pays minimal maintenance, and only agreed to do so after the humiliating procedure of a paternity test. He wants nothing to do with Noah.

When I have spoken to people in a similar position to James's, they've told me that they like their life as it is. They feel threatened and scared by the possibility of it changing if they were to acknowledge the importance of a dependant.

And yet a child – who is not an 'it' but a person in your life, albeit one who is dependent on you for a couple of decades – is more than a mere catalyst for change. If you were to look at becoming a parent selfishly, a child is in fact a source of enrichment.

Also, a child does not cease to exist just because they are being ignored. Sadly, some men (and women) do distance themselves from their children. It's as though, if they pretend they have nothing to do with them, they do not really exist. Mel instinctively knew that she must not tell Noah his father had let her down, even though she felt he had. If her son asks about him, she remembers his dad's many good qualities and talents and tells her son about them. If, in the future, Noah's father should ever want to re-enter his life, Mel being positive about him will help this process. As Noah gets older and asks more questions, it's becoming harder for her. She is worried that her son, when he does know the whole story, will take his father's desertion personally and that it might harm his self-esteem, or maybe distort how he regards his gender, or even negatively influence his own behaviour when he is an adult.

Because Mel is aware of these pitfalls, she can guide Noah around them but, even so, there can be no guarantee he won't at some stage take the fact that his father isn't there for him to heart. Sometimes there isn't a prescription to make everything okay. Mel has a lot of loving and involved family and friends and feels they do go some way to filling in the gap for Noah where a father would have been.

I have told you Mel's story because it's not always easy to conjure up a smooth-running, cooperative relationship with an ex. And when one is lacking, all we can do is try our best not to run down the other parent to our child, or indeed to ourselves.

How to make pain bearable

We want to make our child's life pain-free and worry-free. We certainly don't want them suffering because we were unlucky with our choice of the person we had a relationship with, or because there is conflict in our close relationships. But it's impossible to protect them completely. No life is without angst, unsolved mystery, longing and loss.

How you can make their pain bearable is to be alongside them and with them when they feel it. You need to be present, for your child and the people close to you; open and accepting to what they show you and what they feel. You may not be able to fix their pain, but by being with it rather than denying it or pushing it away, you can keep them company through it. And this kind of attuned company makes anything more bearable. I will say more about this in the part on feelings (see p. 51).

When parents are together

If you are caring for your child with a co-parent, the love, good-will, caring and respect between you will contribute to your child's sense of security. And yet, as anyone who's had a child knows, it puts a strain on your relationship. Spontaneity may be compromised, time alone with your partner or other people you feel close to diminished, time on your own reduced or disappear completely. Your or your partner's relationship with sex may change, and opportunities for sex will happen less often. Sleep patterns will be disrupted and it is likely that you will have to manage on significantly less sleep; each member of a couple, or of a wider extended family, may have different parenting philosophies and the dynamics within the relationships may shift. Your work habits will change and, if you stop paid work, that may alter how you see yourself too. There will be an effect on your social life; there may be less or no contact with former colleagues; some friends may seem to recede for a while due to your preoccupation with your baby; and so on.

And this is by no means an exhaustive list. If you are in a couple, the transition from that partnership to becoming a family takes some getting used to. And just when you think you've got used to it, it changes again, as your child and/or your family continues to grow. These changes can also contribute to the resentment you may experience towards each other and towards your child. By the way, it's better to admit any resentment, even if only to yourself. If you don't, you are more likely to justify acting out of that feeling rather than taking responsibility for it.

Life is never static and being able to accept, work with and embrace change is more useful than resisting it. Thinking about how you can be flexible may be more effective than trying to regain what was lost. This doesn't mean you won't miss your old life sometimes. And it does mean you may need to work at surrendering to your new one and embracing it. Remember Mark on p. 19; he resented the way in which his life was turned upside down by the change from being a couple to becoming a family of three and he learned to accept that change by tracing the source of his resentment to his own upbringing and finding meaning in childcare rather than just writing it off as a boring chore. He also found that when he accepted joint and equal responsibility for his child with his partner, this freed her up to be more of her old self again, rather than being wholly preoccupied with her baby.

How to argue and how not to argue

Most families argue – but it's how you work through any conflict (or don't) and how it's resolved (or not) that matters. Differences in and of themselves do not have to damage a relationship and therefore your child's environment. People with successful partnerships and functional families have disagreements and argue. That's a fact. But when they do they continue to respect and appreciate each other and to have their differences acknowledged and their feelings heard.

Now let's talk about the nuts and bolts of arguing. In any conflict, there is the context. That is what you are arguing about. Then there is how you feel about the conflict and how the other person feels about it. And then there is the process, which is how you go about solving the problem.

To tackle difference, it's important to know how you feel about the context and to share that. The next step is to learn how the other person feels about the context and to take their feelings into consideration. If feelings are left out of it, both sides can get more and more heated as they play what I call 'fact tennis', lobbing reasons over the net to each other, finding more and more to hit the other person with. In this style of arguing, the aim of the conflict becomes to win points rather than find a workable solution. Finding out about differences and working through them is about understanding and compromise, not about winning.

Let's take a typical family argument, about the washing-up. The washing-up is the context, then there's how people feel about it. This is what happens when the process becomes fact tennis:

> SERVER The trouble is, if you leave the washing-up not done, the food hardens on it and it is harder to wash off, so do it straightaway. *15–love*
>
> RESPONDER It is a better use of my time if I leave the washing-up during the day and just do it all together once. *15 all*
>
> SERVER It is unhygienic to leave the washing-up undone. *30–15*
>
> RESPONDER Any accumulated bacteria will be killed when it is eventually washed up. *30 all*
>
> SERVER The dirty dishes attract flies. *40–30*
>
> RESPONDER It's winter. No flies have accumulated around the dirty dishes. *Deuce*

And so on. When one person eventually runs out of reasons and is therefore deemed to have 'lost', they do not feel loving or warm towards their opponent. And if the 'winner' feels good, it's at the expense of their partner.

Another style people use to deal with difference and conflict is what I call 'Look, squirrel!', or distraction. This is when, instead of talking about what is bothering you or someone else, you change the subject. So you see that the washing-up has not been done but, rather than address that problem, you say or do something else. This may be fine – it may be appropriate to delay talking about something – but it is not okay to avoid discussing differences altogether. If all conflict is avoided, what tends to happen is that intimacy is avoided as well, because when too many subjects become taboo, politely skirting around each other can make things lonely.

A third arguing style is being a martyr. This is when you say, as you arrive home, 'Don't worry about the washing-up, I'll do it.' Unfortunately, what tends to happen in situations like this is that the martyr, rather than making everyone feel guilty, eventually becomes resentful and blames other people, or becomes a persecutor (see below) and starts flinging insults.

The persecutor attacks: 'You're a real pig for not doing the washing-up. Your hygiene standards are disgusting.' If you are on the other end of that comment, you feel like attacking back.

None of these four kinds of conflict makes for a great atmosphere in a family home. Conflict puts children on alert, threatens their sense of security and leaves them less able to be open and curious about the world. Instead, their energy and focus are switched into a sort of emergency mode.

What, then, is the ideal way to argue? When working through a difference, work with one issue at a time and think about what the argument is really about. Don't save up your grouches and pour them out on to the other person at once. Start with how the issue makes you feel, not with an attack or by blaming. So, back to the washing-up . . .

'I feel fed up when I come home after having washed up in the morning to see more of it. What would really make me feel better would be if you washed up your stuff during the day.'

The ideal style isn't about winning, it is about understanding. An answer might come back: 'Oh, sorry, darling, I don't want you to feel bad. I had so much work on. I can see it's not a great sight to come home to.' And the response to it might be: 'Yeah, you do have a lot on. Never mind. How about you wash and I'll dry?'

A good rule of thumb when arguing is to do it with 'I-statements', not 'you-statements', for example, 'I feel hurt when you don't answer me when you're on your phone', not 'You're always ignoring me when you're on your phone.' Few of us like to be defined or pigeon-holed – especially negatively – by someone else. If you instead describe how what you hear or see makes you feel, then you are talking about yourself, which is far easier for the other person to hear.

Of course, no way of voicing a complaint is guaranteed to 'work', that is, ensure that you get what you want. But good relating is not about manipulation, it is about having good relationships. Being open about what you feel and what you want can help you to have good relationships, whereas manipulating someone doesn't make for a good connection.

Speaking in I-statements, not you-statements, owning your own feelings and finding out about and acknowledging the other person's feelings are usually the best ways to deal with the inevitable differences that arise in families. It will also help your child feel more secure, as it reduces resentments and promotes understanding. They will also be more likely to adopt this respectful and emotionally intelligent argument style themselves, having had it as their example.

One reason disagreements arise in the first place is when one person thinks they've been attacked on purpose when they haven't. This example happened in a typical family. (I'll call them the Heritage family.)

> Jonny, a twenty-two-year-old student, is inspecting his dad's old leather jacket. He says, 'You're sixty, Dad, you're never going to wear this again. Can I have it?'
>
> Keith, a teacher, has had a bad day of not understanding his son's generation at work, so is feeling old. And Jonny has hit a nerve. Keith raises his voice and says, 'What, can't you even wait for me to be dead before you start eyeing up my possessions?'
>
> Jonny feels like this has come out of nowhere, and now he feels attacked. 'Blimey, I only asked. Why are you always having a go at me?'

'I'm not having a go at you, but I don't like being treated as though I'm already dead.'

This isn't a serious dispute, and I'm pretty certain that Keith will end it by throwing Jonny his jacket and saying, 'You have it, then,' and Jonny saying, 'I don't want it now. You'll need something to wear in your coffin,' and they'll both laugh themselves into a truce. But if they don't understand what went on, they'll both still feel a bit hurt and something similar is liable to happen again.

So, let's see what was really going on by pretending there is a wise mediator there with them.

'He wants me dead,' says Keith.

'No, I don't, I want his jacket,' says Jonny.

'Same thing,' says Keith, realizing at the same time it is not the same thing.

The mediator says, 'It's not the same thing but, today, for you, Keith, it feels like the same thing – and Jonny has no reason to know that. You, Keith, felt attacked. As Jonny didn't realize that you felt attacked, he felt what you saw as your retaliation came from nowhere, so he counter-attacked.'

'That's certainly true for me,' Jonny says.

Keith is quiet, so the mediator says to him, 'Just because you felt attacked, it doesn't mean you were attacked.'

'He called me sixty!' Keith defensively replies.

Mediator: 'Yes, he was hiding his feelings behind a fact, a habit he has picked up from all the "fact tennis" he's been witness to since he was born. Moving on, it seems you find being sixty hard to come to terms with. So you'd quite like to cling to symbols of your youth, like that leather jacket. There's no reason why you shouldn't, and you can say so if it's true.'

A new version of the conversation might sound like this:

'I love your leather jacket. Can I have it?'

'I need some time to think about that . . . I can see you really want it, but I'm not ready to let the jacket go. It's true, I may never wear it again, but I need time to get used to the idea of being as old as I am. And, in the meantime, clinging on to my youthful clothes is a comfort to me.'

'Sorry, my asking reminded you of being sixty.'

'Oh, don't worry, I need reminding. I'm feeling a bit old because I don't understand what some of my students are going on about.'

'Like what?'

'I've just got my head around what social media is, but what do they mean when they say "swipe left" at me?'

'Here, let me show you . . .'

Exercise: Unpack an argument

Think about the last disagreement you had with a loved one. Without getting caught up in who was right or who was wrong, unpack what happened like I did in the example between Jonny and Keith. Then, again as I did in that example, take a meta perspective to see the situation and work out the feelings of each protagonist. Then play the role of a wise mediator and think about how to change the dialogue in the disagreement and how it could have gone better.

Here is a quick recap list of what to remember when you're talking about a difficult subject or when you're getting annoyed or think that an argument is imminent:

1. Acknowledge your feelings and consider the other person's feelings. That means not making yourself 'right' and the other person 'wrong', not making yourself 'clever' and the other person 'stupid'. Nothing wears a relationship or a family down more than if the people within it insist on being the person who is right. Instead of thinking in terms of 'right' and 'wrong', think in terms of how you each feel.

2. Define yourself and not the other, so speak in I-statements and not you-statements.

3. Don't react, reflect. You don't always have to reflect before reacting – I'm not advocating that you lose all spontaneity – but if you feel annoyed or angry, I think it is a good idea to pause and understand why. If Keith had done that in the example above, he would have realized that the anger he felt towards his son when he asked for the jacket did not belong with his son.

4. Embrace your vulnerability, rather than fearing it. In the example above, Keith would also have realized he was scared of growing old and he was about to mask that fear with anger rather than allowing himself to be vulnerable. But it is only by allowing our vulnerability, being open about who we are, that we can have close relationships.

5. Don't assume the intent of the other person. Without assuming too much or projecting yourself on to the other, try to work out what they are feeling too, and admit it if you got it wrong. Understanding your own feelings and those of the person you are negotiating with is not only the cornerstone of negotiations, it is the foundation of functional relationships and of empathic parenting. It is never too late to start this way of interacting.

When parents are able to do all this, I've found that improvements in patterns of relating to one another usually come pretty swiftly.

Fostering goodwill

In a couple or in a family, having the ability to consider each other's feelings requires a store of goodwill. If you feel you're running low, you need to bolster it up.

So, what fosters goodwill? There seem to be two main ways

to do it: (1) responding to bids for connection or attention, and (2) finding solace in each other rather than seeing the other, or others, in the family as adversaries. In other words, both cooperation and collaboration but not competition.

When psychologist John Gottman and his colleague Robert Levenson set up what they called the Love Lab at the University of Washington in 1986, one of their experiments was to ask couples to talk about their relationship: to discuss a disagreement they had had with each other, to talk about how they met and a positive memory they shared.

While the couples had these conversations they were wired up so that their stress levels could be measured.

All couples appeared to be calm on the outside, however, the results of the stress test showed something completely different. Only some of the couples had in fact been calm. Others had high heart rates, sweated a lot and generally showed all the signs of being in fight-or-flight mode.

But the real revelation came six years later, at the follow-up session. All the high-stress couples had either split up or were still together but in a dysfunctional relationship. Gottman called these couples the 'Disasters'. The ones who had shown no stress during their initial interview he called the 'Masters'.

It appeared from the data that the Disasters each experienced the other as a sort of threat – more like an adversary than a friend. Gottman studied thousands of couples over a long period of time and found that the higher the couple's stress indicators, the closer they were to being Disasters and the more likely they were to split up or have a dysfunctional partnership.

So, what do these findings mean? The more you feel stressed and threatened in the company of your partner, the more likely you are to act in a hostile or cold manner towards them. The more your relationship is based on getting one up on them, on winning or losing, on being right, the more likely you are to feel hostility rather than goodwill towards your partner. It can be a relationship vicious circle. One-upmanship is all too common in our culture as a way of being together. Even advertising seems to rely for its success on making the target market feel superior to others; this is second only to making the target consumer feel sexually desirable. I'm thinking of the 'dumb dad' advertisements for cleaning products or commercials where the 'prize' for buying a product seems to be that you get to be smug, as if you have somehow been proven to be superior to your partner.

Conversely, when a couple feels calm and soothed by being together, this makes each partner more likely to be warm and affectionate with the other. Gottman set up another experiment where he observed 130 couples socializing together in a holiday home for a day. What he discovered was that when couples are together they make what he refers to as 'bids' for connection. For example, if one partner is reading and says, 'Listen to this,' and the other one puts down their own book ready to listen, their bid for connection has been satisfied. They are looking for a response, a sign of support or interest.

Responding to someone's bid meets their emotional needs. Gottman found that couples who were no longer together after six years (the time of the follow-up session) had on average only a three in ten response rate to such bids. These small, day-to-day interactions generate goodwill and reciprocal treatment, and without them our relationships cannot be sustained. So, this is the key to a successful partnership: be responsive and interested. And what is true for couples is true for all relationships, and especially for those with our children.

As well as responding to requests for attention, there are other things you can choose to do that will foster goodwill – or the opposite. You can look for things to appreciate in your partner, family members and, indeed, in your children. Or, instead, you can scan them for their faults and mistakes. You can choose to express your appreciation or your criticism. I know which I prefer to hear. You can choose to be kind – and the good news is, kindness is catching.

If you are unilaterally kind, research has shown that it is likely that your partner will catch it and pass it on.

Tipping the scales, if they are unbalanced, from being critical to finding things to appreciate is not only crucial in your partnership or in your relationship with your family but in life as a whole. I come from a family where the culture was tipped slightly more towards criticism than appreciation, and I have had to work hard to change that. When I slip back into old habits, it can feel like I'm bathing myself in a toxic soup of criticism.

Being kind is not about being a victim or being unassertive. Being kind does not mean you don't share your feelings when you are angry. What it does mean is explaining how you feel and why but without blaming or insulting the other person.

It is also important to know that just because you did not intend that your actions should cause a family member to be upset or irritated, it does not mean that those actions did not upset them. When someone feels bad in response to something we may have said or done, even unintentionally, it is important to listen and to validate how they feel rather than become defensive. We need to remember that we all experience the same things differently. No one is wrong because their experience is different from what ours would be. Such differences need to be respected rather than causing you to get into arguments as to who is having the 'right' experience.

There's lots of advice out there. Some of it will tell you not to sweat the small stuff in families and relationships. Others counsel the exact opposite and advise dealing with minor irritations before they become big. The main thing I believe we should aim for is understanding how the other person feels, even if we feel differently, and feeling for them where they're at and, hopefully, being felt for in our turn. Everyone benefits from being listened to, understood and empathized with. Make this a priority in your family. It will make your family a good place for a baby to land and a good environment for a child to develop in.

Exercise: Notice attention bids

Become more aware when members of your family make a bid for your attention or connection and, if possible, turn towards that bid rather than turning away. This is whether the bid comes from your partner, your mother or your children. Relationships are precious, and turning towards bids is a major part of relationship maintenance.

Although we are individuals, we are also very much part of a system and a product of our environment. As we have seen in this part of the book, there are several things we can do to help that system and environment be a healthy place for our children to grow.

PART THREE

Feelings

There is nothing like becoming a parent to teach us that human beings feel before they can think and that babies and children are more about their feelings than anything else. How you respond and react to your child's feelings is important because it is a fundamental prerequisite of human beings – big and small, you and me – to have our feelings witnessed and understood by the significant people in our lives.

A baby is pure feeling – a bundle of feelings, if you like. We won't always understand everything they feel, we'll sometimes have to soothe them for a long time before they feel soothed, but it is by putting in such loving work that you will build the foundations for your baby's future emotional health. If you take their feelings seriously in their first few years, the baby will learn that if something feels bad, it will get better, especially if they can share how they feel with someone sympathetic.

You responding sensitively to your child's feelings teaches your baby or child to have a healthy relationship with how they feel, whatever they are feeling, from the extremes of rage and grief, through contentment and feeling calm and relaxed, to the highs of joy and generosity. This is the basis of good mental health, and that's why this section is probably the most important one in the book.

Learning how to contain feelings

Ignoring or denying a child's feelings is potentially harmful to their future mental health. I know that you, as parents, might not even know you're doing this, or maybe you do it because you think it's for the best. When other people, especially our children, are unhappy, denying their difficult feelings is sometimes our default option. It can feel like the right thing to do. It might feel right to try to belittle, advise, distract or even scold the feelings out of them. We don't want the person we love to be unhappy, and being fully open to their unhappiness or their rage can feel dangerous and unsettling for us; it can even feel as if we are encouraging these feelings in some way. But when feelings are disallowed they do not disappear. They merely go into hiding, where they fester and cause trouble later on in life. Think about this: when do you need to shout the loudest? It is when you are not heard. Feelings need to be heard.

I do not want you to feel bad about how you might have reacted to your child's feelings in the past, but I do want to emphasize how vital it is to acknowledge, take seriously and validate your child's feelings. The most common cause of adult depression is not what's happening to the adult in the present but because, as a child, they did not learn in their relationship with their parents how they can be soothed. If, instead of being understood and comforted, the individual was told not to feel, or cried themselves to sleep alone, or was left by themselves with their rage, their capacity to tolerate unpleasant or painful emotion becomes less and less possible as the number of emotional misattunements adds up. Their capacity to tolerate them diminishes. It is as though there is only so much space for difficult emotions to be pushed down into before that space gets too full and there is nowhere for them to go. When we are soothed, and soothed again, by our parents, whatever our feelings, we are liable to feel more optimistic about those feelings, which makes us less susceptible to depression or anxiety later on in life. There is no guaranteed way to avoid mental-health difficulties, but it certainly helps to instil in us a belief that, whatever emotion we experience, we are still acceptable and, however bad we may feel, it will pass.

Remember: all parents make mistakes, and it is putting these right that matters more than the mistakes themselves. So, if you have thought that the best policy for making your child feel better is to pretend not to notice when they are angry or unhappy, do not worry. You can change this pattern of how you respond to your child's feelings so that they do feel seen and heard. It is likely to feel strange or even alien when you begin to act in this new way, but it can easily become your habitual way of responding. First, think about how you have responded to your child's feelings in the past. There are three main ways – and your way can often be similar to how you respond to your own feelings. You may vary between the three, depending on the emotion or the situation.

Repressing

If you are a repressor, your natural inclination is to push away strong feelings and say, 'Shush,' when you are confronted with them, or 'Don't make a fuss, nothing's the matter,' or 'Be brave.'

If you dismiss a child's feeling as unimportant, they are less liable to share any subsequent feeling with you, whether or not you might consider these to be unimportant.

Overreacting

On the other end of the scale, you might be feeling so much for the child that you become as hysterical as they are and cry along with them, as though their pain is yours rather than theirs. This is an easy mistake to make, for example in the first few days that you drop your child off at nursery, before you both get used to it.

If you take over a child's feelings like this, they are also less likely to want to share how they feel with you. They may think that they are too much for you, or that you invade them by merging with their feelings.

Containing

Containing means that you can acknowledge and validate all your feelings. If you can do this for yourself, you'll find it natural to do this for your child as well. You can take a feeling seriously without overreacting and remain contained and optimistic. You might say, 'Oh dear, you are unhappy. Would you like a cuddle? Come to me, then. There we are, I'm going to hold you until you feel better.'

If a child knows they will be seen and soothed but not judged by you, they are more likely to tell you what is going on for them.

This is what a child needs: for a parent to be a container for their emotions. This means you are alongside them and know and accept what they feel but you are not being overwhelmed by their feelings. This is one of the things psychotherapists do for their clients.

Being able to be a container means witnessing anger in a child, understanding why they are angry and perhaps putting that into words for them, finding acceptable ways for them to express their anger and not being punitive or overwhelmed by the anger. The same is true for other emotions too.

We are all different when it comes to which emotions we are more comfortable with because of our own experiences in childhood. It depends what associations with each emotion were made by other people and so by us as we were growing up. If you grew up in a family who habitually have contact with each other through conflict, you might have become inured to raised voices or even shouting; indeed, they may even have associations of love for you. If, on the other hand, you come from a family who shied away from any confrontation, you may be deeply uncomfortable with anger. If you felt manipulated when you were growing up, you may distrust or feel uneasy with warmth and love because you expect it to be accompanied by a sting.

Exercise: How comfortable are you with your emotions?

This exercise is a good way to begin looking at your usual reactions to emotions, in both yourself and your child. One at a time, think about fear, love, anger, excitement, guilt, sadness and joy. Which emotions do you feel more comfortable with? Which ones make you feel less comfortable? Which are easier for you to cope with in yourself? And how about when they are directed towards you, or when you witness them in other people?

We need emotions, even inconvenient ones. Think about the inconvenient ones as warning lights on a dashboard. Your response to the petrol warning light flashing on empty should not be to remove the bulb so it doesn't flash but to give the car what it needs in order to run better. And so it is with feelings. In the main, we should try not to be distracted away from them, or to deaden them, but instead to heed them and use them to work out what we need so that we can be aware of what we want, and, if appropriate, go for it.

The importance of validating feelings

Our feelings come into everything we do and every single decision we make. How we manage our feelings will have a bearing on how our baby or child learns to manage theirs. Feelings and instincts are closely linked, and if we deny how a child feels we are in danger of dulling their instincts. And a child's instincts make them safer. For example, in the excellent book *How to Talk so Kids Will Listen and Listen so Kids Will Talk*, the authors tell a story of a child who goes with her friends to the local pool but comes home very soon after she left. 'Why are you back so soon and on your own?' asks the mum. The daughter explains there was an older boy at the pool who wanted to pretend to be a doggy and lick their feet. Her friends thought it was funny, but it made her feel icky. I believe it is quite likely that her friends had been trained not to react to certain things by their parents saying, 'Don't be silly, don't make a fuss,' rather than being encouraged to take their feelings seriously. If this was the case, it will have compromised their safety. It is too easy to dismiss a child's fears about, say, trying a new food, but if we tell them not to be silly rather than listening to them, there is a danger that they will think they are being silly to feel what they do, when it isn't silly at all.

Goodness, you may be thinking, it is hard enough to do all the practical things I need to do to keep my child safe, fed and clean. Now, as if that wasn't enough, I need to feel with them too? But as much as I hate 'tips' and 'life hacks', if there is one big hack, it is this: do not get into a battle about what a child is feeling. Your eight-year-old might say: 'I don't want to go to school.' Replying 'You are going, and that's that' is something that can easily come out of your mouth when you're in a rush and have your own agenda to worry about. But saying 'You really hate school right now, don't you?' is easier for your child to hear. It opens up the dialogue rather than shutting it down.

And it is very rarely quicker to deny a child's feelings. For example, we are often in a hurry, so we grab a toddler to try to put their coat on, and they do not like it. Then we ask them to put their coat on themselves but, by that time, they're determined not to put it on. So, you see, it would have been better to put the time in first by respecting them and acknowledging their feelings. That means not grabbing them but warning them that it's time to put their coat on, then observing, listening and reflecting what they feel back to them. If they refuse to put their coat on, you might say, 'You hate being too hot, that's why you don't want to wear your coat. Okay, we'll put it on once we are outside and you start to feel cold.' And if you are always in a hurry in the mornings, get up earlier to give yourself the time to respect your child's slower pace and to acknowledge their feelings. Then life is less likely to be a battle.

One mother, Kate, told me that when her child, Pierre, was a toddler, a few times a day something would upset him and he'd cry.

> It was often something which to me seemed really minor, like the fact it was raining or he had had a little fall, or I told him swimming with the penguins at the zoo isn't allowed. I tried to be understanding because I knew that what for me felt minor could easily feel like a catastrophe to a toddler. But by the time he was four, and it was still happening, I was beginning to think Pierre would never build up any resilience. I started to think I might be being too soft. And that perhaps I should start telling him he was making a fuss about nothing. What stopped me doing that was remembering how bad I felt when my parents told me off for being silly or that I needed to grow up.
>
> Now Pierre is six, and I've realized we often go days and days without a tear. What, before, would have had him in floods of tears, he now deals with. He might say, 'Never mind, Mummy, we can figure this out.' Or 'Give me a hug while my knee stings. It will stop in a minute.' The change happened gradually and imperceptibly. I'm so glad I kept on accepting his feelings and soothing him.

Although it probably seemed extremely time-consuming at the time, Kate did choose the most expedient path. When we tell our children off for feeling bad we are giving them two things to cry about: the thing they were originally sad about and, in addition, they now feel bad because their parent is cross and they still feel sad. Stick with the philosophy of soothing the tears, feeling *with* rather than *dealing with*. If you take a child's feelings seriously and soothe them when they need it, they will gradually learn to internalize that soothing and eventually become able to do it for themselves.

If you were brought up being disapproved of for having

inconvenient feelings, it is all too easy to revert to that same model with your own child. One thing that may stop you making that mistake is remembering back to when you were made to feel bad for feeling sad, like Kate did. Feeling sad is part of life. But if being told off for feeling sad is still within you, even as an adult, you may find yourself apologizing for crying when something awful has happened.

It can be hard to accept your child's feelings rather than telling them off for expressing them if, like Kate, your feelings were denied by your parents. It can feel like taking a leap into the unknown, and you are, it's true: you are breaking the links in your ancestral emotional chain. But remember, you are laying down the foundation for your child's good mental health. By the way, slip-ups in either under- or overreacting, especially when they are mostly corrected, are not going to ruin a child for ever.

Becoming comfortable with your own emotions, however strong, is the key to being able to contain and soothe your child's. If you dismiss your own feelings as unimportant, you will not be able to be an adequate container for your child's emotions. If you become hysterical, you are unable even to contain your own feelings, let alone your child's.

You may need to practise dealing with your own emotions, not repressing them or becoming hysterical but acknowledging how you feel and finding ways of soothing yourself or accepting help from those around you to help you soothe yourself. One way of doing this is to define your feeling rather than yourself. You can do the same for your child. So rather than saying, 'I am sad,' or 'You are sad,' say instead, 'I feel sad,' or 'It looks as though you may be feeling sad.' Using this language means you define the feeling rather than identifying with it. This small thing can make a big difference.

It's also important to be in the habit of talking about feelings, both yours and your child's. As children mature, the logical part of the brain becomes more dominant. It's not that they become solely logical – human beings will always be emotional – but they can learn to use pictures, drawing and language to talk about and understand how they feel. By doing this, their feelings start to work for them, rather than them being at the mercy of the feelings. When your child expresses feelings it can help to order and make sense of them if you put them into words or pictures.

It's easy to say, 'You seem happy about that,' but it can feel harder to acknowledge difficult feelings, or feelings you wish your children did not have. If a child is crying because you've said no to ice cream before lunch, acknowledging difficult feelings doesn't mean you give them ice cream, or that you give up work so they never have to go to the childminder again or give in to whatever it is they are unhappy about. It just means you take their feelings seriously, you take them into consideration when making decisions and you help to soothe the feelings, not by denial or distraction but by acknowledgement, understanding and not running away and distancing yourself from them. It can feel risky at first to acknowledge feelings you would rather they did not have – such as hating their sibling or visiting Granny – but if your child feels seen and understood, it does give them one less thing to protest and cry about.

In his book, *The Orchid and the Dandelion*, published in January 2019, Dr Tom Boyce talks about how he and his fellow researchers were collecting data to see how the stress of starting school affected children's immune systems, when the 1989 Californian earthquake happened. At first, the researchers were dismayed because this extra stressor would jeopardize their study, but they decided to capitalize on it by researching the effect of the earthquake on the children's immune systems. All the children were sent a packet of crayons and some paper and asked to 'draw the earthquake'. Some children drew happy, cheery pictures of the disaster, while others showed more distress in their drawings and illustrated the dire aspects of the earthquake. Which group of children would you expect stayed the more healthy after the earthquake? The kids that drew happy, optimistic pictures of the earthquake sustained substantially more respiratory illnesses than the ones who depicted fear, fire, fatalities and disaster. Dr Boyce took this to mean that the human trait that stretches back throughout history, of expression through telling stories, through making art, is a way of taking ownership of the things that scare us, because the more we express ourselves about these things, gradually, the less scary they become. We express our sadness, although it may hurt to do so, because each time we express it the sadness, to a greater or lesser extent, diminishes.

In the book Dr Boyce talks about how some children are ultra-sensitive and their environment impacts them a lot. These he calls the Orchids. Other children are naturally more robust, and he calls these the Dandelions. There is no knowing really whether your baby is a Dandelion or an Orchid, but Dandelions benefit from having their feelings listened to as well. It is essential that parents are sensitive to an Orchid's feelings, and all of us, whether Dandelion or Orchid, benefit from having our feelings seen, validated and understood – even if, in the same circumstances, we would have a different reaction.

The following case study is about an Orchid child called Lucas whose parents, like most families these days, both needed to work. These days, not many families have the luxury of one parent staying at home who is always available for their family, and it can feel unfulfilling to stay at home if that does not suit your temperament. A child will prefer to have happier parents than miserable martyred ones, and so I am not at all saying that one parent must stay at home, what I am saying is allow your children to have their feelings about their world, about any domestic arrangements and not be in denial about them. This is because not only will a child have more capacity for happiness if all their feelings are allowed, not just the convenient ones, but, if Dr Boyce's interpretation of his 1989 earthquake study are correct, by being able to express how they feel and have those feelings listened to and understood, they'll also have stronger immune systems. We want our children to be happy so desperately, because we love them so much, we can fall into the trap of our being in denial about how our children are feeling. I am hoping that Dr Boyce's study and the following story will remind us that this is not the wisest course of action.

The danger of disallowing feelings: a case study

Annis and John are warm, kind people, devoted to each other and to their young son, Lucas, aged ten. They both own their own small businesses and have worked extremely hard at building up their reputations and their client bases. They have bought a flat and feel happy that they will have this investment as part of their future security but they continually feel financially insecure.

Lucas started nursery when he was small but never settled. So his parents employed a series of au pairs to look after him. In their financial situation, they didn't feel they had any other choice but to have childcare. The au pairs would take Lucas to school, collect him and be there for him in the school holidays. In between au pairs, friends and Lucas's granny would help out. Annis and John made sure they had time together as a family at weekends, and Lucas seemed happy enough. They each always held Lucas in mind by thinking about him and loving and caring for him, and they looked forward to seeing him, although often by the time they got home he was already asleep. If Lucas asked to see more of them, they would promise to take him for a treat at the weekend. Lucas seemed fine.

Yes, Lucas seemed fine, until, aged ten, he attempted to jump out of the window, six storeys up. He was prevented from doing so only because John had forgotten something so returned to the flat and managed to pull him back in. The au pair had been washing up in the kitchen. Now, I know this is alarming to hear, and I must stress that it is unusual for a child in reasonably happy circumstances like Lucas to try to kill themselves.

Lucas's parents took time off work to be with him because they knew it was an emergency. They had had no idea that Lucas was so distressed. 'I think,' John told me, 'we only saw what we wanted to see.' John was also unsure about using the anti-depressant drugs their GP was talking about. He had a gut feeling something must be wrong, and numbing Lucas's feelings with medication didn't seem right to him. He took Lucas to a private therapist. Sometimes Lucas went to see the therapist alone, sometimes with one or other of his parents. Lucas talked to the therapist about the days he had in the holidays when he was shipped about from friends' houses to Granny's and then back home to an au pair. He felt like a nuisance because he heard his parents on the phone trying to organize the care for him, and it seemed so hard for them. On one level, he knew his parents loved him because they told him, but it was hard for him to feel loved. 'Some days,' he said, 'I just feel like Pass the Parcel.'

He also told the therapist how he'd get fond of one au pair, only for them to leave and be replaced by another. Then he felt bad because he began to forget some of them, even though he had really liked them. And that made him feel they must have forgotten him too.

He couldn't remember when he started to feel sad; he didn't even know he felt sad. When he'd tried to tell Annis and John about how he was feeling, they had found it hard to listen so they'd tried to distract him or cheer him up, or flat-out contradict him.

As parents, we want more than anything for our children to be happy. So when they aren't we want to convince them, and ourselves, that they are. This may make us feel better in the short term, but it makes our children feel unheard, unseen and lonely.

John: Before, if Lucas said or showed he wasn't happy, I'd say something like, 'Don't be sad – we're going to the zoo on Saturday,' or 'I'm buying you a new games console.' Working it through with the therapist, we found out that he experienced that as me telling him off. I'd want to say, 'I'm not!', but the therapist would gently stop me, ask me to validate what Lucas was saying.

It felt that if I acknowledged to Lucas that, say, me not being there when he gets back from school makes him sad, I would be making him sadder. That was hard. But because we'd had such a massive wake-up call, we really did have to make changes, so we did what the therapist said.

When Lucas said he felt sad, I learned to ask him what it felt like, or where he felt it, or whether he knew why. When we accepted his feelings, he felt heard rather than pushed away, and that, to my surprise, did make him feel better.

We also learned that it's not enough to tell Lucas we love him. We need to show him he is our priority. And he is – that's why we work so hard. We need to show him we love him by being with him properly, not just saying, 'Night, night,' on Skype or taking him on weekend treats.

I got a loan so I could spend a month at home with Lucas. We hung out, watched cartoons, went to the therapist. Lucas didn't talk much but, when he did, I listened. The therapist taught me to listen without having to fix, and I tried to put that in place that month.

Lucas is back at school now. We make sure at least one of us is home by 6 p.m. so he gets a good two hours of being the number-one priority with one of us every evening. We make dinner together, play together or just watch TV together. I'd like to say I never look at my phone during those two hours. I try not to.

Annis has found it all a lot harder. She feels so bad that she hadn't realized how awful Lucas felt, scared they could have lost him or that he might have badly injured himself.

Parental guilt does not help us or our children; acknowledging our errors and making changes does. As I will keep emphasizing throughout this book, none of us is perfect and we all make mistakes. It is not the mistakes that matter so much, it's how we put them right. The ruptures that cause problems in our relationships with our children and their mental health are only a problem if they are not repaired. I also want to emphasize what the therapist and Lucas found out was that it was not so much that both his parents went to work that was the problem but that he felt so very alone with how he felt about it. Just like with the children who lived through the earthquake – it was not the earthquake that made some of the children ill, but it was the children who could fully express how they felt about the disaster whose immune systems kept them safer.

I expect Annis's guilt may have something to do with traditional gender roles, that she felt herself to be more responsible than John for Lucas. Of course, parents are equally responsible for their children, but it is hard to throw off the traditions of generations. That does not mean they should not be thrown off. These things need discussion so different members of a family are not assuming different things.

I hope Annis will be able to feel good in the future because both she and John realized what they'd been doing to contribute to how Lucas felt and they put it right. They both learned how to validate feelings and experiences, and they are great at doing this for Lucas now, as well as for themselves and for each other.

Thank goodness, most children do not attempt suicide. But do not wait for wake-up calls, whether it's getting into trouble at school, anger issues, self-harm, depression or anxiety, to demonstrate to your child every day that you hold them in mind and that their feelings are to be taken seriously. Encourage them to draw how they feel or say how they feel and then accept those feelings. It is important to show them that what they feel matters.

Words, on their own, only go so far; deeds go further. You cannot delegate love – a certain amount of child-minding, yes, but love, no. Nor can you procrastinate about giving that love: it won't wait until the weekend; children need it from at least one parent every day. The child psychiatrist and psychoanalyst Donald Winnicott noticed when watching children play Hide and Seek that 'It is a joy to be hidden, and disaster not to be found.' This is also true in life. We may like some secrets, as adults and as children, but if no one truly sees and meets us as we are, where we are, and when we want it, it can lead to disaster.

Rupture and repair and feelings

When thinking about feelings, keep remembering about rupture and repair. I wish I could say that I never spoke harshly to my child, or that I never put my own feelings before my child's – of course I did, like my parents had done before me. But the difference between how I was brought up and how my daughter was brought up is that my parents never admitted to being unjustified or wrong. Even when I was an adult child, my parents never apologized if they treated me unfairly or were proved to have been mistaken about something. I knew I did not like this, so I made a conscious decision not to repeat it.

Despite my good intentions, on occasion, I behaved in a way I regretted. When I did, if I caught myself, or realized later on, I would always apologize to my daughter, or change how I thought or went about something. My daughter's father and I made changes when our behaviour wasn't helping and we confessed to our daughter when we'd slipped up. I did not know how this would affect her. It was an experiment – creating a new link in the emotional family chain. But I began to find out quite early on.

One afternoon when Flo was about four years old she was eating a piece of cake in the kitchen, and she said, 'Sorry I was grumpy in the car, Mum, I was hungry. I'm okay now.' She was saying sorry. She was reflecting on her behaviour and trying to repair a perceived rupture. I was thrilled. I never expected that taking responsibility for my own bad behaviour, not justifying it or blaming someone else, would mean she would learn to do the same.

But, of course, she would. Children, like the rest of us, tend to do as they are done to. Being sensitive to feelings and following rupture with repair is always better than stand-offs, battlegrounds and winning and losing.

Another time I remember being thrilled was the first time my daughter said, 'I'm going to get angry soon.' Instead of acting out on her anger, she was putting it into words. I was able to say to her, 'Yes, it's really annoying, isn't it?' And she learned to carry on talking about how she felt rather than having a tantrum.

Felt with, not dealt with

Dave, father of Nova, aged four, was frustrated that she seemed to cling on to her routines. He hated how she could get into a full-blown tantrum when she did not get her way, for example if she couldn't sit in her favourite place in the car. He'd argue with her or cajole her to be more flexible, but they usually ended up just being very cross with each other.

Dave asked me what to do to help Nova learn to be adaptable

and I explained the importance of validating feelings. He decided to give it a try:

> Some of Nova's cousins needed a ride, and one, unknowingly, sat in Nova's usual seat. She started to cry. I'd usually have said either, 'Don't make a fuss, just sit somewhere else,' or asked her cousin to move. But what I did was crouch down so we were on the same level and say softly and gently to her, 'It's really hard for you to see Max in your seat. You really want to sit there, don't you?' Her crying subsided a bit and she looked back at me. I really felt for her and I felt that she saw it in my face. I told her she'd be able to sit there next time. And I asked, 'Where do you want to sit now, by the window or on the booster seat in the front?' To my surprise, she went and fetched the booster seat and strapped herself in and began happily chatting.

Telling Nova off and cajoling her had just been making her more stubborn. When she saw that her dad really did feel sorry for her, she no longer needed to keep clinging to her point. Dave validated Nova's feelings. Like steering into a skid when you're driving on ice, if you steer away, the car keeps skidding in the same direction, but if you steer into it, aligning the wheels with the direction of travel, you regain control of the car – and then you can steer out of the skid.

One of the hardest times to acknowledge your child's feelings is when you feel differently. For example, maybe your seven-year-old child sighs deeply and says, 'We never go out.' You may feel like countering, 'But we went to Legoland just last week!' or 'We go out all the time.' You may feel angry that the effort and expense of taking your child to a theme park seems to have gone unappreciated.

Denying your child's feelings can start to alienate this person with whom you want a loving, life-long relationship, this person whose happiness you really care about. Changing your reaction might feel counter-intuitive, but all of us feel better when our experience is acknowledged and not argued with, and children are no exception. Realize that your child is only telling you what they feel and use this as an opportunity to connect with them, to talk about their feelings rather than pushing them away.

Denying unhappiness doesn't make it go away, it just digs it in a layer deeper. Let us go back to our example.

CHILD   We never go out.
ADULT   You sound bored and fed up.
CHILD   Yeah, we've been indoors all day.
ADULT   That's true, we have. What would you like to do?
CHILD   I'd like to go back to Legoland again.
ADULT   That was fun, wasn't it?
CHILD   Yeah.

The child is more likely to feel satisfied with this conversation, and it's less likely to escalate into an argument. Your child isn't daft – they know they can't be in Legoland every day – but they need their parent to know they want to be with them and to feel this with them. It's about soothing their feelings as they learn the unpleasant lesson that life does not always go their way.

This is true for everyone, child and adult. When we feel bad, we don't need to be fixed. We want to be felt with rather than dealt with. We want someone else to understand how we feel so we do not feel lonely with that feeling.

My daughter, Flo, now an adult, told me the other day, 'I feel so ashamed for failing my driving test.' No one likes to see their child in pain and it's easy to make the mistake of rushing in to try to fix it. 'You don't need to feel ashamed,' I said, desperately trying to fix her. 'No,' she replied. 'I just need a hug.'

We all slip up, like I still do, but if we do feeling-with rather than trying to push the feeling away enough, the child will know what they need and be able to ask for it.

You do not have to wait until your child can talk to validate their feelings and take them seriously. You can do it by reading the situation, how you think the child is feeling, and putting that into words. Even when a child can talk they may not be able to articulate a feeling as well as you can, which is why, in the example above, the child describes how they feel as 'We never go out' rather than the reality of 'I feel restless, cooped up and at a loss to know what to do with myself.' The parent puts into words the feelings they observe the child having, which resonates with the child and leads to a moment of connection, when they reply, 'Yeah . . .'

Monsters under the bed

When they are very small, children may talk of ghosts or monsters under the bed. Rather than paying attention to the story or the reason they give, pay attention to the feeling they are expressing. Instead of dismissing the idea that there are monsters under the bed out of hand, name the feeling the monsters seem to be representing. 'You sound scared, can you tell me a bit more?' Or, 'Let's make up a story about these monsters. What are their names?' If you do this, you may be able to vanquish the monsters. Do whatever fits your natural style; it isn't so much the words we use, it's staying with our children until they feel soothed rather than dismissing them as silly. For all you know, those monsters may be representing your impatience at bedtime or something else complicated that your child can't articulate. Even when it's impossible to trace the source of every feeling, that doesn't mean the feeling isn't real. It still needs validating.

And making your child feel silly with a 'Don't be silly – you know monsters are made up' is unlikely to soothe them.

What's important is to keep the lines of communication open. If you dismiss your child by telling them they're being silly, they learn not only to clam up on the 'silly' communications but also those you wouldn't consider silly.

The distinction between 'silly' and 'not silly' is so clear to us we might assume it is to a child as well. But nobody can help feeling what they feel, even if other people would feel differently in the same situation, even if other people think it is silly.

You want to be the person your child can talk to. If you tell them they are being silly to complain when Granny made them a nice lentil stew, they may feel they can't tell you when the creepy piano teacher puts his hand on their leg. The difference between those two things is loud and clear to us but to a child they are both filed under 'something icky'. And if some icky things are dismissed as irrelevant by you, your child is likely to feel it is not worth the humiliation of sharing any more of them.

You may think this is an extreme example because Granny's stew and a piano teacher touching a child's leg are so very different. But your child has not been in the world as long as you have, has not had all your experience, has not read everything you have read, has not yet understood sexuality. Your child may not have learned to register alarm at being touched inappropriately in the same way as they feel alarmed about eating something they don't like. To them, both are an assault on their senses. Telling a child they are being silly about anything will close down communications from them to you, and that might be a dangerous thing to do.

The importance of accepting every mood

If someone asked you what you'd wish for your child, you'd probably reply, 'I want them to be happy.' It is no bad thing to want your children to have a capacity for happiness. But do we perhaps have too much invested in the idea of 'happy', in a perfect picture of your family having a perfect time, gambolling in the meadow, having a lovely picnic among the wild flowers?

Happiness, like all feelings, comes and goes. In fact, if you were happy all the time, you'd hardly know it because you wouldn't have other emotional states to compare it to. And for a child to be happy it's necessary for parents to accept all their moods and all aspects of how they experience their world. It will be no picnic for much of the time.

It isn't possible to be scolded, or even distracted, into happiness. The more fully you accept and love your child no matter what their experience is and how they feel about it, the more capacity for happiness they will have. This goes for you as well as for your children. We need to accept ourselves and all our moods as well.

I remember one of my parents' friends asked me, when I was twelve years old, whether I was having a happy childhood. I told him, 'No, not really, no. I do not feel particularly happy much of the time.' My father overheard this and turned angrily to remonstrate with me. 'What nonsense,' he said. 'You have an idyllic childhood, a very happy childhood. What rubbish.' And, because he was my father – my beloved, if scary, father – I felt I must have been mistaken. I felt confused, unsure of my own feelings.

Parents tend to take it for granted that what they think would make them happy will make their children happy, but this isn't necessarily the case – as you have most likely found out. You may feel like a failure if your child seems unhappy and rather than feeling such an uncomfortable feeling, you may, like my father, have tried to scold your children into happiness.

If I knew then what I know now, when my father contradicted me I would have been able to make more sense of what I was feeling, but at the time my brain just went into an unclear, confused fug. It's the fug I feel when I feel something but someone I look up to tells me I do not have that emotion. And in the fug there was also shame, because I had got something – I was never clear what – wrong, and wrong again.

What my father missed was an opportunity to connect with me, maybe not at that moment but after his guest had gone. He could have asked me what I was feeling and not taken the answer, whatever it may have been, as though it were an attack on him. He could have helped me to articulate it and he could have tried to see the world as I saw it. I'm not saying he had to change his view of the world, but he could have tried to see that my viewpoint too was a valid way of seeing things and of seeing myself.

If you treat your child's sadness, anger and fears not as negatives to be corrected but as opportunities to learn more about them and to connect with them, then you will deepen your bond with them. Then, there is every likelihood you will increase their capacity for happiness.

If you came home and said to your partner, 'I had a foul day at work,' and they replied, 'It can't have been that bad,' you probably wouldn't feel seen, heard or met by them. You might even feel batted away. If this is the sort of response you habitually get, you might give up confiding in them.

If your partner said instead, 'Tell me about it,' and you did, if you told them how unfair your boss had been and how you had to do everything twice because of her carelessness, and if they said, 'No wonder you feel you had a bad day,' you might begin to feel a bit better.

If, on the other hand, your partner started their reply with something like, 'Well, you should . . .' and gave you advice, you would probably feel worse. If your partner replied by saying, 'Look at that cute squirrel out of the window,' you might well stop talking about work, because what would be the point of going on and saying any more? The squirrel might help you forget you are unhappy, but the feelings, not having been worked through, would return.

Remember this: when your baby, or your child, your adult child or even your partner confides a painful feeling, although it might feel that you are making it worse by acknowledging it, you will in fact be helping them work through their emotions and so making it better.

It may be easy enough to be sympathetic with your child about a bad day at school. But what if you really do not like what they are saying? For example: 'I don't like the baby, I want you to take her back to the hospital.' Then, it is even more important to listen, to try to understand and to validate how they feel. Say, 'You have really been missing out on time with just you and me lately, no wonder you want the baby to go away,' or, 'It's not fair that all the visitors coo over the baby and seem to not pay enough attention to you.' Or even, 'What does it feel like now you are a brother?' Whatever the answer, accept it. You cannot tell a child that they love their sibling. They are aware of how they feel and they need a safe container for those feelings.

The demand to be happy

The psychoanalyst Adam Phillips said that the demand that we be happy undermines our lives. Every life involves pain and pleasure and if we try to banish pain and drown it out with pleasure, or otherwise numb it or distract ourselves or someone else from it, then we don't learn to accept it and modify it.

People often have goals in life and assume attaining these goals will make them 'happy'. Sometimes they may, but often our assumptions about what will make for a satisfying life are wrong. We can be unconsciously led astray by pictures of smiling, laughing, attractive people amid wonderful architecture, gleaming cars and beautiful objects, and such images condition us to assume, without putting anything into words, that this is what we want. There are no advertisements showing ordinary-looking people working through their demons, learning to accept inevitable pain and finding their spontaneity and joy in that way.

This is a truth that should be universally acknowledged: when you try to block out a 'negative' feeling, you remove positive feelings too. As therapist Jerry Hyde says, 'Emotions don't have a mixing board – they just have a master volume. You can't fade out sadness and pain and fade up happiness and joy. You turn one down, they all go down.'

Before our babies and children are exposed to the culture of pleasure through things, they have a better idea of what is satisfying – and that is connection. It's a feeling of being understood – 'got', if you like – by their parents and caregivers and finding sense and meaning in their environment and so feeling connected with it. To be 'got', a child needs us to accept all their feelings, their anger, fear, sadness and their joys. We are ill equipped to do this unless we are connected to our own feelings.

When you are wishing for your child's happiness, despite what the gods of consumerism have drilled into our skulls, this is probably not about having stuff. Nor is it about being the cleverest, the richest, the tallest, or the shiniest, or anything else. It is about the quality of their relationships.

The way we learn to relate to our parents and siblings is habit-forming, a blueprint for all our later relationships. If we get into a groove of having to be right, having to be the best, having to have material things, having to hide how we really feel, not having our thoughts and feelings accepted as they occur, these types of dynamics can put a brake on developing our aptitude for intimacy and our capacity for happiness. But validating our children's feelings strengthens the bond between us and our child.

Hilary is a single parent who runs a hairdressing business.

> Tashi was three when her little brother Natham was born and I did the thing I was told to do, buying her a present from

the baby. But she was not fooled by that. 'A little baby hasn't got any money and can't go to the shops,' she said. At first, she revelled in being told she was a big sister now and proudly told visitors that. But after a while the novelty of having a new baby in the house wore thin for her and she began having more tantrums, refusing to cooperate, started wetting the bed again. All through this, with my mistaken good intentions, I told her she loved being a big sister. But her behaviour just got worse and worse.

One night, I was thinking it over after an exhausting and, to be frank, perfectly horrible bedtime. I thought back to when my own little sister was born and how I'd hated it – and how I'd thought I was a very bad person for hating her. Then, as we got older, I knew I was a very bad person because everyone told me I was when I was horrible to her – but I couldn't help it. I felt it was me or her. If I'm honest, I can still be irritated by my sister for no particular reason.

I realized that trying to force Tashi into liking Natham was working no better for her than it had for me. I began to feel sorry for her. I decided I'd really try to understand her feelings and articulate them to her and I'd keep doing it for as long as it took to make a connection, because I was feeling so far apart from her.

The next morning, I said, 'You really hate Natham being here, don't you?' She didn't say anything. And I went on, 'I remember when your auntie was born, I really hated it too. And just like I have been doing to you, everyone told me I must love it, and I didn't. I'm sorry, Tashi, that you are having such a hard time of it.'

That day, when she played up, I didn't tell her off, I just kept it up: 'You don't like it when I've got to feed the baby instead of playing with you. Sorry, Tashi.' Whenever she had to share me or wait for something or be inconvenienced, I described how I thought she must feel about it.

Tashi didn't cheer up immediately but by teatime her behaviour had improved. We felt closer again because I wasn't fighting her feelings, I was going with them. It was great to get her cooperation back. She even started to help, fetching nappies and passing wipes and telling me when Natham woke up from his nap. That night we had the first dry night since Natham was born.

What I learned is, when a child feels something, no matter how inconvenient, no matter how much I might want to deny it, I need to name the feeling, check with them I've got it right and validate how they are feeling. The other day we had to leave the park and Natham, who's now three, wanted one last go under the fountains after I had just dried him off – which would have meant he'd be soaking wet in the car. My mum tried to persuade him he didn't want to be wet in the car, but he wasn't buying it. I stopped her and said to Natham, 'You really want to get wet again, don't you? I'm sorry you're disappointed.' She was amazed how he accepted this.

I'm also pleased to report that, although there are squabbles between Natham and Tashi, most of the time they either play together or separately without animosity.

Exercise: Feel for someone else

Practising feeling how somebody else feels will make it easier to do when a real situation arises. Think about a person or a group of people who have come to a different conclusion to you about something – say, for example, they vote differently to you. Rather than dismissing them as stupid, think about their circumstances, their hopes, their fears. Put yourself in their shoes and try to understand why they have reached a different decision to you. Feel with them about how they feel.

Empathy is harder work than it may at first seem. It is not about giving up your own point of view but about truly seeing and understanding why the other feels as they do and, most importantly, feeling with them.

Distracting away from feelings

Distraction is a tactic favoured by parents to divert children from having whatever experience they may be having. It's commonly used, but it's rarely appropriate. That's because distraction is a trick and, in the long term, being manipulated will not help your child develop a capacity for happiness.

Look into a baby's eyes and you'll see nothing but sincerity. I believe our children, whatever their age, deserve nothing less from us. Distraction is not sincere on the part of the parent and it is manipulative. It can also be an insult to a child's intelligence.

What message does distraction convey? Imagine you fall over and badly graze your knee. How would you feel if your partner, instead of being concerned or interested in the pain or the blood or the embarrassment, pointed out a squirrel or promised that you could play your favourite video game?

I'm not saying there is no place for distraction, but not as a manipulative tactic. If, for example, your child needs to have a medical procedure, it may be a good idea to tell them they will feel it less if, instead of concentrating on the injection, they concentrate on the sensation of your fingers stroking their forehead. In this example, you are not trying to trick them – they know what is going to happen – you're offering distraction as a comfort.

Your children are liable to treat you in whatever manner you treat them. You would not like it if you asked to discuss their school report with them and they pointed out of the window and said, 'Look! Squirrel!'

It is also a good idea to tell your child's nursery teachers and childminders that you would prefer it if your child's feelings were empathized with rather than something they were distracted from. Distracting a child away from a toy another child is holding to ward off a conflict will not help them to understand, and nor will it help them learn how to negotiate a struggle. Avoiding difficult feelings is not how we learn how to deal with them.

Besides, if your child wants something you do not want them to have, like your car key, say, they need to learn they cannot have it rather than just being temporarily distracted away from it. They need to hear that you don't like them playing with your key rather than hearing you say something like 'Ooooh, look at this dolly.' You can help them with their frustration rather than distracting them from it by saying, 'You are angry that I can't let you have the key. I can hear you are furious about it.' If you stay calm and contain your child's feelings, this is how they will learn to contain them. It might feel like a longer process than simply distracting them away from the key, but the time invested will help them internalize these skills for themselves.

If you repeatedly distract your child from what they feel or from their experience, you are also unwittingly discouraging them from being able to concentrate. Think of it like this: if your child has hurt themselves, or had their feelings hurt or their wishes denied, if you distract them from what they feel rather than help them work through it, it will discourage them from holding their attention on difficult things. And you do not want your child to be easily distracted from doing a difficult task.

But I believe the worst thing of all about unwanted distraction is that it's a bar to a good, open and close relationship with your child.

One of the reasons you might be tempted to make light of what a child is going through by distracting them from it or denying their feelings is because you see the situation through your eyes, not theirs.

For example, if you as an adult cannot go to work with your mother, it's not the end of the world. But for a toddler, it may feel as though it is. We may also be feeling guilty about being the cause of their distress so it may feel more comfortable to deny it.

So, what do you do if one partner goes out to work and your toddler seems inconsolable about it? If you are the parent who's leaving, leave with confidence. Your child will be more likely to feel secure if you are calm, firm and optimistic. It is important not to sneak out but to take your leave with concern and kindness. If you panic about going, you may become overdramatic, and this won't help your child. If you ignore their hurt, you are not being the mirror for them you need to be. Acknowledge what they feel; give them a hug and say something in a kind way like, 'You don't want me to go to work, and I will be back at teatime.'

If you are the parent or carer left with the child, what you need to do is be with the child where they are emotionally. This means acknowledging what has happened, which may be: 'You didn't want Mum to go out. You feel sad.' If you think about it, it is entirely appropriate that you should be sad when someone you love leaves. You can say when she will be back. 'Mum will be back by teatime.' Do not lie about how long someone will be gone. The child will either learn a distorted idea of time or just not believe you on the next occasion.

Be there for the child, be attentive and be mindful about your own discomfort. Be concerned, but do not overreact. Stay calm and do not leave the child alone to cry. Do not distract the child or 'shush' them or tell them they aren't feeling what they are. Keep on listening, offer a hug if it is wanted. After a while the child may find an activity or you may suggest one, but not while they are deep in their distress. Remember how it might feel if you were missing someone you love so much you feel you cannot survive without them and another person comes along and pushes your deep, heartfelt feelings aside rather than respecting them. Once you have expressed yourself, when you are becoming resigned to the situation you will become more open to a suggested activity. That's very different to someone ordering you to look at Action Man doing a funny dance while you are in the middle of your distress.

Exercise: Think about distraction

Think about occasions when you have felt upset. How much time did you need to put your feelings into words, to try to make sense of them and get used to them, before you were ready to distract yourself by watching a film or reading a book? Just because the things we and our children get upset about are different, it does not mean their feelings are any less intense or real than ours.

A baby can't help but be their feelings. In time, a child can learn to observe their feelings as a way of containing them – but they cannot learn to do this alone. They need someone to accept and hold all their feelings as they grow up.

In our great need of wanting our children to be happy, sometimes we push them away when they are angry or sad. But for good mental health, children need to have their feelings accepted and to learn acceptable ways of expressing all their feelings – and the same is true for us adults. So, it is important to accept our own feelings rather than denying them, and essential to accept our children with whatever they may be feeling too. By helping a child put their feelings into words (or pictures) we help them to process them as well as to find acceptable ways for them to communicate what they feel.

PART FOUR

Laying a Foundation

Pregnancy

It may seem strange to put a chapter about the very beginning of becoming a parent – about pregnancy – some way into this book. But even if your child has already been born, or indeed is a teenager or an adult, this chapter may throw some light on your relationship and why it is where it is. If there is something in your relationship with your child that feels stuck, the ideas in this chapter may help to repair it. If you are near the beginning of your relationship with your child, it may help to steer you in the direction of the loving lifelong relationship we all want.

I often see parents thinking they can treat children as things to be efficient about, to deal with and fix. It's usually because the parent is busy, life is busy and this is how the parent has learned from their own parents to deal with children. It is a dominant, old-fashioned ideology that promises you can slot parenting easily into your busy life. But too often there is a price. If you don't treat your child as a person, if you have dealt with them rather than felt with them, you might find, when that child becomes a teenager or an adult and you want to have a conversation with them, they are not very forthcoming with you.

You might think the following case study about a thirty-eight-year-old woman and her eighty-one-year-old mother is hardly relevant in a section on pregnancy. But if you haven't done it yet, pregnancy is a good time to reflect on your own relationships with your parents and think about what you wish for your future relationship with your child. You can think about how you're going to aim for one that is honest and open and not confined by roleplay.

We form bonds with our children. Natalie, who told me the following story, does have a bond with her mother. But a bond can be so much more than a filial tie; it can be one of real connection, of liking as well as love. That is what honesty and openness can bring.

'If you met my mother,' said Natalie, 'you'd think she was a perfectly nice woman, charming, even – and she is. It's just I don't feel I'm myself when I'm with her. I feel I ought to go and see Mum more often, but something in me just doesn't want to go. I have to force myself to visit her.'

Something about the relationship as Natalie described it was obviously not working. On a later visit, Natalie got some more insight as to what it might be.

A few years ago, I decided to take what was, for me, a risk with Mum. I thought if I was more real with her, maybe she'd be more real with me. So I told her what I was really feeling, that I'd been having bouts of depression since my partner and I had split up. Mum just said, 'Oh, I have a really happy life.' And that was the end of it.

It clicked: I realized my 'difficult' feelings were unacceptable to her. I think even her own 'difficult' feelings are denied by her. So when I'm low, maybe for her it feels like some sort of threat. I have tried to discuss it, but that emotional door is firmly shut.

I want to be kind to Mum but, after thirty-eight years, our relationship is stuck at arm's length, in the polite-conversation stage. It doesn't seem we can go anywhere else.

When I got pregnant with Brigitte, I knew I didn't want her to visit me when I'm old only out of duty. I want her to want to come – or not – out of choice, and I want her to feel she can be herself and share anything she wants to share with me. I thought about how to do this a lot when I was pregnant. I thought, if I don't feel like myself with Mum, then possibly Mum didn't or doesn't feel like herself with me.

This might seem daft, but I made a resolution not to be fake with Brigitte but to always be myself. When Brigitte was born and I was faced with the forceful sincerity that only a baby can give you, I knew it felt like the right thing to do. I decided to do my damnedest to pay her the compliment of being sincere. Of course, the level of honesty has to be age appropriate, for sure.

I'm really working on being open to and accepting of Brigitte's every mood, not just her smiley ones. And of my own moods too. I now know how hard it can be when you've got a baby who cries a lot and is difficult to calm. When that happens, it brings up all sorts of feelings in me. I feel useless, I feel angry – at three o'clock in the morning I have been known to join in with her and cry too. But I know I'm feeling those things, I accept them and work on acting in a caring and loving way, on treating her in the way that I would like to be looked after if I was that baby in my arms.

I have had to work at not feeling like a failure when I can't cheer Brigitte up. It has sometimes been hard not to frantically try to fix whatever may be wrong, especially when it is not immediately obvious. But instead I try to be with her, alongside her, trying to understand.

I'm not saying it is easy and I'm not saying I manage it all the time, but I talk to her and, when I'm with her, all of me is there. I don't want to be a cut-out parent from a parenting manual, I want to be myself. I hope this will help Brigitte to be able to be all of herself with me when she's older.

As expectant parents, and as parents, the best thing we can do is to take the long view. By this, I mean we should not see our babies, children and teenagers as chores to feed and clean or otherwise fix but as people from the off, people we are going to have lifelong relationships with. This gives us the best chance of making our bonds with them loving and secure.

When you become a parent you begin to form a bond with your baby, a bond that can strengthen with every year. In fact, it's in pregnancy that the foundations for this bond are laid down. Once your child becomes independent from you in practical ways and has their own social network and significant others, this bond can continue to grow as you continue to keep up with each other's lives and concerns.

Sympathetic magic

How do our relationships with our children generally begin? As soon as you announce you're pregnant, you are given a barrage of advice about how to eat, what not to drink – and generally what not to do. The actual advice differs according to the culture and the time, but this process – of being given a lot of advice – is pretty much the same.

Such a large number of rules and advice to be followed may give you the impression that there is such a thing as an optimal pregnancy . . . which may unwittingly lead you to assume there's such a thing as a perfect parent who produces an impeccable child.

I believe this way of thinking may interfere with our relationship with our children, not help it. Believing that pregnancy, childbirth and parenting can be somehow optimized puts us in danger of bringing into the world an object to be perfected rather than a person to relate to. It would be better, rather than giving in to overbearing, impossible perfection, if we realized that pregnancy and parenthood are not projects. They are, instead, as I keep saying, about bringing into the world a person with whom you are going to have a lifelong liking and loving relationship.

There's a second reason you may want to think about how you react to all the rules and advice you may be given about pregnancy. Obeying all the rules and taking all the precautions we're advised to, although some of them may indeed be helpful, can give a false feeling of control over pregnancy or what chromosomes and diseases we pass down to our child.

Think about it like this: there are so many rules about pregnancy, and they vary from culture to culture. But it can really put parents into a panic if they feel they haven't followed the advice they are given to the letter. In the UK, for example, you will be given advice about avoiding unpasteurized milk products. If you digested some before you knew you were pregnant, you may panic that you've contracted some ghastliness that will hurt your baby.

Some risks you will be warned about; some you won't. The reality is, it's impossible to have a completely safe pregnancy. Pregnancy is, by its nature, a risk. You may have a child who is different from most children and therefore does not fit into this draconian category of 'perfect' – but you are creating a person to love, not a work of art.

Some cultures, like the Kaliai people in Papua New Guinea, believe that for a pregnancy to be successful the couple need to have sexual intercourse as much as possible up to and possibly during labour. The Kaliai also believe that if a pregnant woman eats flying fox, a common meal in their culture, the child will be mentally defective or tremble in the way the flying fox shakes.

You'll find such customs and taboos throughout the world. Anthropologists call this 'sympathetic magic': symptoms are connected to something the mother ate or did during her pregnancy or lactation period. Whatever rules you're being told to follow, whether they are scientifically proven medical ones or folklore, they'll be different depending on where you live in the world, and they continue to change. I'm not suggesting you should ignore medical advice, but do consider how it makes you feel.

You might be delighted with this research from Yale University: pregnant women who in the last third of their pregnancy ate five or more portions of chocolate a week had a 40 per cent lower risk of developing pre-eclampsia. And, apparently, there are more reasons to eat chocolate. In 2004, Katri Räikkönen at the University of Helsinki researched the association between the amount of chocolate mothers ate during pregnancy and their baby's behaviour. When the babies were six months old, their behaviour was rated in various categories, including fear, how easily soothed they were, how often they smiled and laughed. The babies born to women who had been eating chocolate daily during pregnancy were more active and smiled and laughed more. They also measured the stress levels of the mothers. The babies of stressed women who consumed chocolate regularly showed less fear in new situations than the babies of stressed women who did not do so.

The trouble with any advice is that, if it comes too late for you, you may feel you've done your baby some harm. The chocolate advice came too late for me. I don't regularly eat chocolate and my baby laughed frequently anyway. Sympathetic magic, be it medically proven or traditional, can be reassuring when we do follow it and panic inducing when we do not. As I said before, we have less control over pregnancy than we may find it comfortable to believe.

Extreme stress (sometimes called toxic stress) caused by trauma, such as ongoing physical danger in pregnancy, does adversely affect the development of the unborn child, as does malnutrition and, of course, we all avoid such things if we can. Normal stress, like having a difficult job or working through our differences with people, will probably not affect your foetus.

There is a risk you might have a child with an abnormality or that the child might not survive. And there is very likely nothing you could have done about this, no magic that could have prevented it, whether it's avoiding eating flying fox or whatever rule you think you have broken.

The sympathetic magic I think is most helpful is to think of your experience of pregnancy as affecting the foetus, as though the environment of the womb is telling the baby a story of what they will find after they are born. So, if you enjoy yourself, feel relaxed, eat well and feel optimistic, the story you will be telling them is one that they, and you, will want to continue after the birth.

One way to begin this story is to notice how being given all this pregnancy advice makes you feel. When appropriate, steer those feelings from fear to optimism. I believe it helps if we don't think about our unborn child as something that might go wrong. I don't think that's the way to necessarily build the best foundation for a mutually satisfying relationship with this new person. We get into habits about the way we think about people, and your foetus is the beginnings of an individual person.

Concentrate on what can go right, not the scary stories you hear. Oh, and the same goes for people's difficult birth stories. Being in a good mood will affect your unborn child. Looking in the direction you want to head in rather than concentrating on where you don't want to go will make your outlook more positive and serve as a better foundation for your relationship. (Besides, if the worst does happen, having been terrified that it might won't alleviate any grief.)

The habit of optimism where our children are concerned is necessary. For their sakes, we need to believe they'll develop and learn and get the hang of things. I know how much easier it is for me to achieve anything when someone I look up to believes in me, and I'm sure I'm not a freak to feel like this. I couldn't have attempted this book, for example, if my literary agent hadn't believed in me. In the same way, your child needs you to believe in them so they can thrive. And you can get into this habit of optimism during pregnancy.

Before you meet a new person you may hear about them from other people. You begin to form a picture of this person before you've even begun to know them for yourself. Think about the influence what you've heard has on what you think about this person. We may like to think that we reserve judgement until we have met them and know them for ourselves but, in my experience, most of us do not.

In her book *Origins*, Annie Murphy Paul describes an experiment in which 120 pregnant women were asked to describe the movements of their foetuses. If the women knew they were expecting a boy or a girl, it made a significant difference to the language they used to describe the movements they felt. Key words used for female foetuses were 'gentle', 'rolling' and 'quiet', whereas for boys the words were 'energetic', 'vigorous' and 'jabbing'. The language of women who didn't know the sex of their baby didn't follow these clichéd patterns. This is just one area we need to be self-aware about in order not to lumber the child with expectations of what they are like before they're here. Instead, we need to get into the habit of observing rather than judging.

How you are thinking about your unborn baby will also influence your future bond with them. If you get into a habit of thinking about your foetus as a parasite, a wilful invader, a burden, or as an imaginary friend, a living god or something in between, it may well make a difference to your later relationship with your child. It will also influence whether you are apprehensive about meeting your baby or, as I hope you are, looking forward to it.

Exercise: How are you thinking about your baby?

Observe yourself as you think about your unborn baby. Think about the way you are thinking about them and how it may influence your future relationship. This will put you in a better position to make a choice about how you begin to relate to this person you have not yet met.

Talk to your foetus, out loud, to help you strengthen your bond. Foetuses can hear from eighteen weeks' gestation. You will hear yourself and understand how you are relating to this person, which can help you become more aware about what you are bringing to this relationship. It will start the habit of talking to your baby once they are born too, as well as the habit of seeing them as another person.

What's your parent tribe?

According to a seminal book first published nearly thirty years ago but which remains as valid now as it was then, there are two main types of parent, regulators and facilitators. In *Psychological Processes of Childbearing*, Joan Raphael-Leff describes how regulators tend to be more adult-centric and routine-led, whereas facilitators are more child-centric and go with the flow of the infant rather than trying to get the infant to fit in with them.

If you're a regulator, you prefer to get your baby into a routine. The regulator philosophy is that children feel safe and secure if the same thing happens at the same time every day, because the child knows what's going to happen and there are no surprises. Parents also know what should happen when and, if they have childcare, the carer sticks to the routine too. People are drawn to this idea if they feel supported by order, by having a structure and knowing what is going to happen and when.

Or you could be a facilitator. They also believe predictability is important for their child, but rather than the routine being predictable they prioritize always giving the baby a predictable response. So the baby gets to know that their cues are responded to and their needs generally met, the idea being that the baby learns that their world is safe and this makes them feel secure.

There isn't much point in arguing which is better, because you will have a leaning towards being one or the other, perhaps because of your culture or in reaction to how you were brought up. And the roles are fluid. With your first child, you may be a facilitator because when there is only one baby to look after you can follow their lead, but when you have another you may need more of a routine so that everyone's needs are met. For example, you cannot let the baby sleep if you have to do the school run with an older child or children; the baby will have to get up and come too.

Sometimes one parent in a partnership may be a facilitator and the other a regulator. If this is the case, it won't be particularly helpful to lob facts backing up your preferred parenting philosophy at each other. Quoting facts and figures and tables and statistics to support your argument is more likely to keep you fixed in your respective corners.

You probably feel your position is based on facts and not your feelings – but we tend to find the facts that fit our feelings rather than the other way around. Discuss it with your partner in terms of your feelings, not facts, trying not to get hooked up on what you think is right or wrong. Feelings are feelings; they are never right or wrong. It may help you to become less entrenched in your position if you admit that you prefer leaning towards a facilitator position or a regulator one because it suits you better rather than believing your position is only for your child's sake.

Whichever philosophy you are more inclined to follow, remember that acceptance, warmth and kindness are the things that matter most when it comes to our children (and most other relationships as well).

Raphael-Leff noticed that those who fall more into the facilitator camp tend to give in to the emotional upheaval of pregnancy, whereas the regulator tends to hold out against it more. She observed that the facilitator becomes more inward-looking, marvelling at the wonder unfurling inside her, while the regulator wants to cling on to her normal persona for as long as possible and tries not to 'give in' to her altered state. She may even feel the pregnancy as invasive. Facilitator types are more inclined to experience their foetus as an imaginary friend.

A facilitator feels that her identity is enhanced by pregnancy, whereas a regulator may feel that her identity is somewhat threatened. Facilitators may regard birth as a mutual transition in life for her and her baby, but a regulator may see birth more as merely a potentially painful event. I mention all these differences to help normalize any feelings you are having. If most of your pregnancy and parenting peers are on the opposite sides of the facilitator/regulator spectrum to you, it can feel lonely.

There are many arguments, customs, traditions, directives and books taking each side to persuade you that one way or the other is better, but what matters – what really matters – is that facilitator or regulator, adult-centric or child-centric, you are honest with your child and with yourself. This means acknowledging your natural inclinations and your feelings. And it means acknowledging that the way you are is because of how you are naturally inclined and how you feel.

Exercise for expectant mothers and fathers

Notice what feelings the experience of becoming a parent is bringing up in you.

Are you running towards being a parent or feeling anxious and wanting to run away from it?

Notice what expectations you are having about becoming a parent. Think about managing these expectations and notice how they are influencing how you are acting. For example, if you are full of worries that begin with 'What if . . . ?', try changing that 'What if . . . ?' into a 'So what if . . .' If you realize you have been assuming that children just need to be tricked into behaving conveniently, challenge that thought and think in terms of relating to them rather than manipulating them. Think about your body as your principle way of communicating with your baby and visualize it becoming familiar and comfortable to your child and your child becoming comfortable to you. Begin to talk to your baby; they can hear you. Look forward to meeting them.

If you are co-parenting, do this exercise and discuss together what it brought up for each of you.

Exercise for existing parents

If, after reading this, you felt your attitude was 'wrong' in pregnancy – for example, you were extremely stressed and emotional, something that can happen not only because of hormones but also because there's more to worry about – forgive yourself immediately. We want to make sense of our world, it gives us a feeling of being in control, but try to make sense of it in a way that does not leave you with a feeling that you have caused a rupture which is now impossible to repair. For example, you may be telling yourself that you or your partner worried so much when you were pregnant that it caused your child's current problems with, say, concentration. There may be no environmental reason why your child is the way they are. Observing them in the present is more useful in working out how best to help them than thinking it is something you did when you were pregnant. Heal that stressful pregnancy by acknowledging you did what you could for yourself at the time with the knowledge and resources you had. Berating yourself will not help anyone.

The baby and you

The next few pages are about the way you meet the baby, the birth and how you might feel in the first few minutes, hours, weeks and months after the birth. Although we would all like to have a calm birth and an instant bond, although this time is sold to us as the biggest and most important moment of our lives, it isn't a fairy story, it's real life. This means things may not go to plan. I would also say there's quite a lot of sympathetic magic needed to make us feel safe, to get us through the birth and the first few days. Get help when you need or want it – no one can do this completely alone – and when it comes to advice, follow that which feels most like reassurance to you rather than that which feels like a leap too far. Being guided by that will allow you to be in your life as it is and not make you feel like something is wrong just because life is not measuring up to a perfect ideal.

Making your birth plan

You've probably thought about the type of birth you think would suit you, whether that's one with all the pain relief going, one where you float in a pool, or something in the middle.

And it is worth taking the time to do some research. Plan whatever to you seems the most desirable and the least traumatic, as that's what's more likely to get you and your baby off to a good start.

As I'm sure you've heard from other women's stories, your baby's birth may not necessarily stick to your plan. A planned epidural may turn out not to be possible and a natural birth may end up as an emergency Caesarean. But planning may get you nearer to the birth you feel you want, so long as you stay flexible about possible, necessary changes to that plan. It's a bit like planning the life you want: all you can do is steer in the direction you want to go and then be flexible about what you cannot control.

When I was pregnant, I wanted a calm, natural, peaceful birth and I made a birth plan accordingly. Yes, I really would have liked that, but my daughter's birth was one that went off plan. The baby's heartbeat dipped – the cord was wrapped three times around her neck – so the lights had to go on and the baby had to be pulled out by ventouse extraction, quickly. But many peaceful birth plans do work out.

My baby had to be whisked off to a special-care unit. I felt a sense of loss that she and I were not having the skin-on-skin contact I believed (and still believe) to be so important. But, we were both alive. It turned out there was nothing wrong with her but precautions were taken because there might have been. As soon as I could stand, I found the unit and met my daughter. Try as they might, the staff could not make me leave. I have told this story many times and I have needed to, because I found her birth traumatic. Now, over twenty-five years later, I can tell it without becoming emotional – but it took a while.

Debriefing from the birthing experience

When we do get a live baby at the end of pregnancy and birth there is a feeling we should be grateful, however traumatic the birth experience. But I believe that as well as being grateful it's important to debrief from the experience, and as often as you need to, in order to regain a sense of equilibrium. This might be part of the reason why, when you're pregnant, you may hear more scary birth stories than ones that went smoothly – because people may need to debrief more from these births.

Becoming a parent for the first time can be overwhelming in itself, never mind getting over whatever experiences you go through giving birth. Even if it is a beautiful, wonderful experience, it can also feel like a momentous event and so it's one you need to talk through.

Some mothers feel guilty about or let down by their birthing experiences. But remember, there is no such thing as perfect. All of life is about getting back on course each time the path takes an undesirable turn. It isn't what goes wrong that matters so much as how we make things right again. And you're getting back on track as you learn to get to know your baby and form that bond.

I don't know whether the separation after my daughter's birth increased my anxiety as a new mother or whether it made my baby more fretful in those early months. Perhaps we would have been like that without the upset of separation immediately after her birth. But I do know that, in those early months, it sometimes seemed as if my baby was hard to soothe, and I was anxious about that. It seemed to me that she was born distressed. By gradually learning how to soothe her, I did find myself somewhat soothed in the process. So, if the birth was traumatizing for her (and it was for me) then in time that rupture was repaired for both of us.

The breast crawl

We are, when it comes to our children, often in a hurry. We're in a hurry to go into labour, to speed up labour, for the baby to breastfeed, to sleep through the night, to wean, sit up, stand up, walk and talk, be independent, get on the property ladder, save for retirement. But if we hold back to observe what our babies can do, we can learn not to be in a rush and our children can teach us to live more in the present.

There is an incredible example of this that happens just after birth. Babies have a seeking mechanism for the breast and can find it with less help than you might have thought. It's called the breast crawl. Widström and others at the Karolinska Institute in Sweden researched this and found that when a newborn is placed on the mother's abdomen directly after the birth the baby can find the mother's breast all on their own. For an average of fifteen minutes nothing much happens, then the baby uses their legs to propel themselves into position, alternating bursts of activity with rest.

At about thirty-five minutes, the baby first puts their hand to their mouth and their gripping reflex allows them to reach for the nipple and stimulate it. At forty-five minutes, sucking and rooting movements begin. And at fifty-five minutes, the infant spontaneously finds the nipple and starts to suckle. These results have been repeated in subsequent studies. Apparently, if the mother has amniotic fluid on her breast, the baby can find their way there even more easily.

It is not surprising babies are born with this instinctive drive to seek out the nipple because it's the norm for other baby mammals. Like other animals, babies have a variety of natural reflexes facilitating our survival in the world, with one of the most obvious being able to cry to tell you they need your company or to be changed, held and fed.

A further study has shown that babies kept on their mothers' bodies in skin-to-skin contact cry far less than those kept in a cot next to their mothers. After twenty-five minutes, those babies who had skin-on-skin contact cried for an average of just sixty seconds, whereas for those in cots it was just over eighteen minutes. Fifty-five to sixty minutes later, the babies allowed to breast crawl with continuous skin-to-skin contact were not crying at all, whereas the control group cried for over sixteen minutes. After eighty-five to ninety minutes, babies with skin-to-skin contact cried on average for just ten seconds, compared to over twelve minutes for the group kept mostly in cots.

It's as though our babies can do this stuff as naturally as any mammal but we have been too keen to interfere with the process. There are other things that may interfere with it too, such as pain-relieving drugs or a Caesarean birth. So many, many babies, probably including you and me, have been denied this self-propelling, natural start in life . . . and some of us have still turned out to be, on the whole, well balanced, fully functioning, loving people who can form wonderful, lifelong bonds and friendships.

What breast-crawl research and practice can show us is that it's okay to watch our babies and learn about what they can do and what they need by observing them. When we watch them we can take our cues from them, in more of a natural rhythm of give and take rather than merely doing stuff to them. To allow a baby to follow their instinct to do their own breast crawl or any other natural action, like gazing at you, crying for you, is to respect them and to trust them and from the start to help them to know that they are not an object that things are just done to but a person who has agency. A person who is in a relationship with you.

The initial bond

Throughout your pregnancy, your body has been telling your baby your story and the story of your environment, through what you have been feeling, what you've eaten, the sounds that surround you and which come from your body. Once your baby is on the outside of your body, that story continues.

Many parents feel an instant connection and rush of love for their newborn, like Emma.

> I was worried I wouldn't bond with my baby, John, as I've never been particularly interested in anyone else's. But as soon as he was put on me I knew he was gorgeous and I loved him fiercely. My labour lasted ten hours. I walked a lot and I used a birthing stool, which worked for me. It was painful but, as contractions come in waves, I did get a rest between each one. I think knowing to expect that helped a lot. I had a bit of gas and air towards the end. After John was born I felt sorry for the other mothers because their babies weren't as beautiful as mine! I didn't realize, because it felt such a special and unique experience, that most mothers think and feel as I did. I didn't know the other mothers were probably idolizing their own infant and pitying me!

A reaction like Emma's is probably due to a rush of the 'love hormone' oxytocin. Some drugs given during birth, or being shocked or traumatized by the birth, may interfere with the release of oxytocin – which may mean that this rush of love, as Emma describes it, is absent for you.

That was Mia's experience.

> My baby, Lucca, was induced. The birth was extremely pain-ful, the worst pain I have ever had. I couldn't have an epidural because the anaesthetist couldn't get the needle in.
>
> When Lucca was born, I didn't feel anything except shock. My mother was with me, and I made her hold him because, I don't know why, I just wasn't ready. Then he was taken to the special-care baby unit for a day.
>
> Those first two weeks I had difficulty even believing he was my son. I seriously thought about having a DNA test because I was sure he had got mixed up at the unit. Anyway, thank god for Mum. She listened to me and my worries calmly and didn't argue with what I felt. And she told me I wouldn't always feel like that. Mum stayed with us for a month. She'd say things like, 'Oh, Lucca has your eyes,' and 'He's so like you were as a baby.' And gradually I began to bond with him.
>
> It wasn't until Lucca was about six months old that I feel our bond really cemented. I was holding him in the pool at a baby swimming class and he was hitting the water with his fist. He looked up at me and laughed – and we laughed together.
>
> Those first few months were hard, I can't lie. I felt I was 'acting as if' we were bonded and it got me through, but it also got me down.

Don't believe that you are a freak or somehow the 'only one' who feels how you feel after the birth. What you need is some-one to listen to and accept how you feel so you can accept your feelings too. You need to accept where you are rather than berate yourself for not being where you think you should be. This was key in Mia's progress in forming a bond with Lucca. Mia's mother did not argue with her or tell her she was wrong to feel how she did but simply acknowledged it.

Exercise: How does your baby feel?

Lie on the floor. Imagine what it is like to feel lonely, hungry, thirsty, uncomfortable in this position yet to have no words – no words to think with and no words to communicate with. Imagine what it is like just to be body and feelings, unable to sit up or roll over or feel that you belong. All you can do is lie there and be your feelings. Now imagine what it feels like to be rescued, to be picked up, made comfortable, held close and to feel part of someone else, although you still have no words, no past, no future, just now and body and feelings.

Support: to parent we need to be parented in turn

It can feel hard to give time, respect and warm responsiveness to a child when you're running on empty. It may be just because you are exhausted right now, or because it feels like those things weren't given to you by your parents. To parent we need to have been parented in turn. That said, you will probably be amazed just how many reserves you'll find and how long it is possible to keep going. But this is not indefinitely sustainable so, if you do feel depleted, get support.

That support might be in terms of practical help to free you up to give more attention to your child – or to sleep. Or it might be having someone listen to you and feel with you while you are in the midst of giving what you feel you were not given or have not got to give. Being listened to, being heard, not being judged for whatever feelings parenting brings up for you do not necessarily need to be done by a trained therapist. Friends and family can be good for this too, if they can accept and relate to normal parental ambiguity. We need to remember it is not our feelings or the things we find ourselves imagining that can harm our children, it is how we act towards them. Think about Mark's case study (see p. 19). The fact that he wanted to run away didn't adversely affect his son because he didn't run away.

This is Charlotte's story:

> I used to have really scary thoughts about hurting my baby, Rosanne. When she wouldn't stop waking me up during the night with crying, I had thoughts of throwing her or shaking her. These thoughts upset me more than her crying did. I felt really ashamed of them and thought, if I told anyone, Rosanne would be taken away from me. Then I tortured myself with thinking perhaps she should be taken away. The only time I had anything like it before was when I wanted to kill my parents when I was a teenager. Those thoughts were not as intrusive as the ones I had about my daughter, though. I really thought I might lose it and hurt her. When I couldn't stand it any more I plucked up my courage and talked to my sister. She told me that everyone feels like that at times and what she does is just watch herself have the thoughts, just like listening to an annoying person you have no intention of being influenced by. Just having her accept me as normal and not think I was going mad really helped, and I think the thoughts of hurting my daughter started to lose their grip on me after this. And I know I can talk to my sister again if they were to come back. I wish I'd spoken about it earlier.

If, as a parent, we feel we can't talk about less-than-ideal thoughts, feelings or imaginings, they can become bigger and harder to manage. It is important to be able to talk about them, to have a place to dispel feelings in a cathartic way, so we don't act them out at the expense of our children.

The sort of support you need is someone who really hears you, who gets what you mean and can take on board all your feelings without being overwhelmed by them so that person acts as a sort of calm container for them. Their calmness comes from the knowledge that, whatever you're going through in terms of anxiety or doom, it will pass. Their gentle optimism can carry you through. That is the sort of help that Mia, in the previous section, got from her mother and Charlotte got from her sister.

You need this sort of support because, in turn, the baby needs you to be able to hold all their feelings without being overwhelmed by them. It's your job to offer this kind of supportive relationship to your child. And it's hard to give that sort of attention to anyone unless you're getting some of it too. You may have to spell out to your nearest and dearest that this is the type of help you need.

You may also need practical help. Some people around you may be good at guessing that you do and offering help but, if they aren't, do ask for it. Also, it is not just mothers who need emotional support but fathers too. Humans are not meant to stand alone, mute and strong; we are pack animals, members of a tribe. Get the tribe to help. It is so much harder to finance a family now than it was for the generation before us because buying or renting a home costs many times as much as it did. I believe that, while we wait for the politicians to rectify this unfairness, perhaps the previous generation could help out new parents financially as well as emotionally.

We need help that enables us to form a better bond with our children, not help that allows us to push them away. Sheena's story gives an example of how that can happen and how to get back on track if it does. Sheena, a part-time stylist, already had two children and was pregnant with twins.

When Sheena had a month to go of her pregnancy she was told that one of her twins wasn't thriving and she'd need to be induced. The subsequent birth was traumatic and dangerous both for Sheena and for the babies. One twin, Charlie, was born fine; the other, Ted, required a lot of help and had to be incubated. Sheena stayed in hospital with poorly Ted and Charlie went home. For four weeks, Sheena helped and held Ted until he was well enough to leave hospital. Sheena's partner, Judd, a very successful musician, worked long hours and was often away from home on tour, and either wouldn't, or perhaps felt he couldn't, take extra time off to become more involved in his family at this time. Possibly he also feared that he wouldn't be able to control his emotions if he dwelt on the fact that he had nearly lost his wife and one of his children in childbirth. The often-asserted belief that men have to be 'strong' does, in my opinion, far more harm than good.

When she got home Sheena couldn't quite take on board the fact that she was the mother of twins. She kept on the nursery nurse they'd hired to look after Charlie. She knew Charlie was hers on a cognitive level but didn't really feel as though he was – she saw him as the nanny's and Ted as hers. Because this felt so uncomfortable, she wanted to forget it and believe that nothing was wrong.

Sheena distracted herself by showing everyone just how fine she was. She went out a lot, regularly clubbing until the small hours. Her feelings kept hitting her like shocks – the shock of having twins, the shock of a very difficult birth, the shock of nearly losing Ted and, worst of all, the feeling Charlie was not really hers. When she felt one of these shocks, rather than looking into it, she got more childcare and distracted herself by going out.

When Charlie cried she never really felt like comforting him. If the nanny wasn't around, she'd ask one of the children, Judd, her mother, the cleaner – 'Anyone but me,' she said later. Her way of comforting him was to try to distract him rather than soothing him through any distress – not unlike how she was trying to distract herself from being overwhelmed by her own feelings.

It wasn't until Charlie was about four years old that, emotionally, Sheena could accept him as her son. 'I think I was in shock for over three years, but I only realized this when I started to come out of it,' she says.

What affect has all this had on Charlie? Now, the twins are ten years old. Sheena's other children, including Ted, are happy-go-lucky, but Charlie is an anxious child and very clingy. He seems to feel he cannot take any relationship for granted and that, to be lovable, he must work hard. Sheena says Charlie would do anything for Ted, even though Ted does not return the compliment, or at least, hasn't yet returned it. Sometimes friends and siblings experience Charlie's wanting to please as neediness and find it annoying. This compounds his problem and then he tries even harder to get it right for other people. This insecurity he has about relationships in all likelihood has something to do with the early separation from his mother and the lack of bonding after her return. Sheena says the only time he is more relaxed is when she spends one-on-one time with him – no easy feat when you have a job and four children.

But once a week Sheena and Charlie go to an art class, just the two of them. Sheena says it's helping. When the art class doesn't meet because of holidays she makes sure they have their two hours every week at exactly the same time, to do art together, just the two of them.

I asked Sheena what might have helped her to do things differently, early on. She felt that, had the birth been less traumatic, she might not have been in so much shock, which she thinks is one reason she went into denial about being a mother of twins. But she thinks the main cause of the rupture was not being with Charlie for those four weeks after the birth. When she got home, she says, 'He didn't smell like my baby, but Ted did.' She also thinks if she'd had counselling at the time she would've been able to face up to what had happened and talk through the impact it had on her. Although Charlie was crying and wanted to be found by Sheena, she too needed to be understood and to be found. By not being able to feel for herself, she was impaired when it came to feeling for others, especially for Charlie. Not feeling for him made it easy for her to distract herself and run away from him, to leave him in the care of the nanny.

Sheena loves and adores her Charlie these days, relishing her one-to-one time with him. By spending as much time as she can with him, she is mending the early rupture. When we are bringing up our children we can only do our best, and, as I keep repeating, to have good relationships with our children it is not so much the ruptures that count but how they are repaired.

Now Sheena and Charlie's bond is cementing, Charlie's sense of security in his relationships is improving. As his sense of longing diminishes, his sense of joy will increase. Because the good news is that, although we are never again the sponges we were as babies, we are not made of stone. We form in relationship with others and we can re-form in relationship with others as well, for the rest of our lives. If Sheena hadn't addressed this early rupture with Charlie, it's possible that, when he got older, his romantic attachments might have taken on the same pattern of feeling insecure, and love to him would have felt more like the pain of longing rather than joyful union.

One day, Charlie may need more help to become more trusting in relationships and less anguished. He may need his parents to tell him the story of his early life so he can make sense of the way he feels. It will help him to know that the way he feels is not because of any fault of his, and certainly not because he is less lovable than anyone else, but because when we are babies we are so very impressionable.

Sheena's partner, Judd, didn't notice she hadn't bonded with Charlie. And he didn't attempt to bond with Charlie either. Had he taken on the role of a primary carer from Charlie's birth, rather than completely relying on the nursery nurse to fulfil all

Charlie's needs, I believe Charlie would have felt more secure in his relationships. I am all for extra help, but children need a primary bond with their parents.

I'm not telling this story so we can tut-tut at Sheena and Judd. He was just doing what the men in his family, and many men in the past, have always done – leaving the early parenting to mothers and to paid help. It is hard to break these cultural patterns because they are so entrenched, unless we are sufficiently aware of them to challenge them.

Sheena probably learned her pattern of dealing with her difficult feelings by distraction rather than working through them because it was how her early caregivers had tried to cheer her up. Just as her husband believed that parenting is not a man's role, it's easy to believe a way of acting is 'natural', whereas it is merely indoctrinated. And these indoctrinations can get in the way of our relationships with our children. It's not a matter of being a 'bad' parent or a 'good' parent – everyone does their best. But if we can make ourselves aware of as many of the effects and beliefs of our culture and our upbringing as we can, we can make repairs that lead to a more functional way of going forward.

Most parents need help with their children, from relatives or paid helpers, so they can work, or even just take a shower. However, the most important people in a child's life should be their parents (and remember: by 'parent', I mean the person or people who have the primary responsibility for the child, so 'parent' may mean foster parent, adoptive parents, step-parent, guardian, surrogate parents, rather than people who temporarily help with this responsibility). Everyone needs a primary bond as a safe anchor in their life. Paid helpers leave, and this can break the primary bond, which may have effects later on. And children need to feel they are a priority for their parents, especially in their early years. They need to feel like they're people to relate to rather than tasks to be delegated.

Exercise: What support do you need?

Write your name or draw a symbol to represent you in the middle of a piece of paper. Around you, write or draw your support network. Think about who will support you naturally and who you will have to ask. For example, your mother may show up and ask the right questions and listen and offer to pay your rent for a year; your sister may cook you meals with the minimum of fuss; your partner may help to keep you company, the home clean and the family financially afloat. Other help may need organizing, for example, starting or joining a group of other parents in a similar position to you or getting professional support if you need it. Draw your diagram using solid lines from support to you if it will just happen naturally and dotted lines if you will have to arrange it. Think about the types of support you might need – emotional and practical. Look for any gaps on your support diagram, then take steps to fill them.

And parents may need support not just after the birth of a baby but at any time while their children are dependent. So this exercise can be repeated every couple of years so that you can ensure you get the help you need to help you make the best possible relationships with your children.

Attachment theory

What's it like, being a baby?

You have a huge advantage over your baby; you have some idea what to expect from becoming a parent. You may have watched your parents look after younger siblings, you will have witnessed other parents with their children, you may remember how you felt as a child, you may have read parenting blogs and books and, most importantly, you have been a baby. Your experience will be consigned to unconscious memory, but it will still be there.

A baby, on the other hand, has no idea what it's like to be a parent. They haven't even been a baby before. Everything a baby experiences is a first experience. It is almost impossible to imagine what that's like, but try to bear it in mind. The first experience of anything forms the deepest impression. These days, as adults, we have fewer opportunities for first impressions. When we meet a new person we get an impression of that person, but it will not do much to change our philosophy of people in general, consolidated long ago.

If you go on holiday to a new place and the people happen to be lovely and the weather just how you like it, that place will probably have good associations and you will think of it fondly. In the same way, life will be easier for a baby if their first impression of the world is as a safe and loving place, one where they feel they belong. Whatever calamities befall them in life, they will be less easily knocked off course and they will recover more quickly if they have always felt that they count, they belong and they are lovable. They will either get this feeling from their very earliest caregivers – you – or they will get different messages.

Imagine if you suddenly found yourself in a desert. No food, no shelter, nothing to drink and, worse than all this, completely alone. How would you feel after one hour? After two? Then, what if, in the distance, you saw some people? You would go berserk trying to get their attention. You'd scream and shout and wave. You'd be desperate. Maybe a baby feels a bit like this.

A baby comes from the womb, an environment synchronized by nature to their needs, into the outside world. After their birth the baby must signal to us what their needs are. It is up to us to read the baby's bodily cues to decipher what they need. Every time they manage to communicate and we manage to respond appropriately it is as if that person in the desert managed to get the attention of those people and was rescued.

If being alone in the desert was your first experience of being alive, you would form your world views and your personality by how those people responded to you. Whether that response was attuned or mismatched; whether you had to scream for a long time before you were attended to; whether your needs were quickly understood and met. And, probably more than anything, how long you were left alone without company when you wanted it would lay down a feeling, a mood deep inside yourself, that would become a default way of being for a long time, until enough other experiences happened to change this.

Babies come into the world pre-programmed to form attachments – bonds – to others. Whether people generally have easy, close and loving attachments, or needy, clingy, complicated ones, or whether they find it hard to attach at all or kid themselves they are better off alone, is, according to attachment theory, rooted in how they were related to as babies. The four main styles of forming bonds are: secure attachment style, insecure/ambivalent attachment style, avoidant attachment style and dismissive attachment style. What you want, in your baby, is to foster a 'secure' attachment style. And to do this, it's first worth thinking about the attachment style you had in relation to your caregivers. If you didn't have a secure bond, you will have to be more thoughtful, self-aware and deliberate about how you are with your baby in order to form a bond than if attuned and empathic responding comes naturally to you.

Secure attachment style

If, when you were a baby, your needs for closeness and sustenance were usually consistently met, you're likely to grow up feeling that other people are generally good. This means you can trust people, get on with others, generally feel optimistic and connect easily with others. All this helps you to have a nice life. Thinking you are an okay person and that other people are okay too optimizes your luck in life. It is as though, when you were dropped into the desert, there was always someone there to catch you, you did not have to work very hard to get their attention, they were there for you and very soon you were not alone and did not feel alone.

This is what we like to aim for. Sometimes parents worry because, when babies reach several months old, they can suddenly become clingy. It's very common for them to want only you and not willingly go to other people. It's because they are securely attached – a good thing – but have not yet developed what psychotherapists call 'object permanence'. This is the ability to feel someone or something exists when they cannot see them or it. If you keep meeting your baby's needs regularly, they will develop object permanence sooner or later and this phase will pass. I do not like to give an average age for when this will happen because for some it happens sooner, some later.

Insecure/ambivalent attachment style

If, as an infant, your needs were only inconsistently met, if you often had to scream long and hard to get attention and sometimes even then didn't get it, it's likely the belief you have of the world is that you will be ignored, overlooked and will have to make a lot of noise to be noticed. You will not be able to take companionship for granted. You might not think of yourself as generally an okay person, nor will you assume that most other people are good and trustworthy. It is as though you had to jump up and down a lot in the desert to get those people to pay attention and they often left you and didn't take you with them. Although your first experiences tend to give you your blueprint, it's possible to develop a secure attachment style if a more consistently positive experience happens often enough to supplant the earlier patterns of relating.

Avoidant attachment style

If you were often left to cry it out and a lot of the time no one answered your cries, you tend to give up. Your internal belief system and mantra would become 'I won't get their attention so what's the point of trying?' You wouldn't believe you have influence over other people, you wouldn't expect to be understood by them and you'd grow up seeing yourself as a loner. When the people pass you in the desert, eventually you stop waving to get their attention because you don't see the point – and they probably think that, as you're not waving and crying, you don't need them. The disadvantage of this style is that, in later life, you can't allow other people to get close to you. As with the insecure attachment style, it is possible to work to change an attachment style, with a lot of practice and work.

Dismissive attachment style

Imagine if you were in that desert and the people often did not stop and then, if they did, instead of seeing to your needs, they expected you to meet theirs, or they abused you, didn't give you sustenance, even caused you physical harm. Imagine the effect that would have on your belief system and how you'd learn to relate to other people. You would probably see others as a source of harm and you would develop little or no empathy and a shaky moral conscience.

Exercise: What's your attachment style?

Can you figure out what sort of attachment style you formed in relationship to your caregivers? Can you trace how these attachment patterns were passed down through the generations of your family to you? If you feel you have an insecure attachment style, an avoidant attachment style or a dismissive attachment style, what will you do differently with your baby to what was done to you? If you feel secure in your attachment style, where do you feel that sense of security coming from? How will you replicate it with your baby?

Coercive cries

You probably hear your infant's cries like a demand. This is because a baby's cry is what we call a 'coercive' cry. People and, indeed, all mammals are biologically programmed to respond to a coercive cry – they are essential to the survival of the species. The cry is an alarm, like a zebra in a herd who notices a lion and communicates this to the herd who then immediately react. You cannot help but be pulled to obey it.

A baby's emotions tend not to be subtle; when they are distressed, they sound desperate. That's because they are. It helps if you know that wants and needs are the same thing for an infant. A baby cannot survive without you.

If you try to block out a coercive cry, you will have to shut down parts of yourself to do it, to go against your nature. You will also be jeopardizing the development of your baby because intimate companionship is vital to babies and vital for your bond together. Their brains do not develop on their own but in relationship with other brains in their environment. Our brains don't stop developing in relationship with those around us until the day we die, but those early days, early months and early years are when most connections are formed and so babies need us to be around and available to relate to.

If you weren't automatically and naturally responded to, surrendering to this process of hearing and responding to the coercive cry will bring up feelings for you. I repeat this warning rather a lot, but if you do feel anything along the spectrum of unsettled to despairing in response to becoming a parent, find support. You do need someone to contain these feelings for you, not to be overwhelmed by them, so you can in turn contain the feelings of your baby.

When babies feel unheld and unmet in their distress what seems to happen is that they dissociate, cut themselves off from it. They may stop crying but, as studies of babies left on their own to teach them to sleep without company have shown, their cortisol levels remain as high as they were when they were crying. Dissociating from distress is a mammalian survival mechanism, a reflex, but the downside to it is that people can experience flashbacks to those feelings they cut off from. Dissociating from a memory leaves people without any control over when they access it, and it can come to haunt them as though it had come out of nowhere.

If you're having difficult feelings as a parent, you may wonder why. It's because having a child of your own can trigger any feelings you dissociated from as a child, which may be uncomfortable, disconcerting, distracting and strange. The triggers may be subtle, but you can be triggered just the same.

If you train your baby not to cry by not responding to them, what you are doing is causing the baby to dissociate from their feelings. They may seem generally fine, but what can happen is that these feelings may surface later in childhood and/or adulthood. I don't think this is a risk worth taking, especially as there's no risk attached to responding to a coercive cry.

If you left your baby to cry for long periods when they were little because you thought it was the best thing for them and for you, what I've written may be frightening or angering you. It won't do any good to beat yourself – or me – up about it. What you can do to repair the situation is to start to take your child's moods seriously, not dismiss them as unimportant or silly, and to keep your child close when they want to be close. You can even tell them what you did and why you did it and that it wasn't their fault. If they are haunted by difficult feelings that seem to come out of nowhere and which they cannot understand, telling them may help them make sense of how they feel. Being taken seriously for what they feel is healing whatever age a child (or an adult) is, and if the person taking you seriously is your parent and they are not defensive and blaming, is powerful medicine indeed.

We can never synchronize ourselves to our baby as perfectly as nature synchronizes the womb. There will inevitably be misunderstandings and ruptures. What we can do is attempt, as far as we can, to care for, respond and react appropriately to facilitate the development of our children's sense of security and to make the transition from being in utero to being on the outside as smooth as we can. Those cries you hear are nature's coercive cries. Loneliness is a feeling like discomfort, thirst or hunger that needs attending to for an individual to keep healthy.

Different hormones, a different you

During pregnancy and after the birth it can feel as if everything you felt before has been multiplied by ten. Victoria is nine months pregnant with her second child: 'I was watching the Winter Olympics speed skating and the woman I was rooting for fell over and crashed out of the race. I burst into tears. That is not me. I am not usually this emotional.'

Well, it might not have been you, Victoria, but it is you now. If you feel things more than you are used to feeling them, don't assume there's something wrong with you. It's not that you're going mad. And although your feelings may seem exaggerated, it doesn't mean they don't matter or that what you feel charged up about is not significant for you. For example, being upset about seeing a sportswoman doing her best and then crashing anyway may be a metaphor for your own anxieties so the cry you have about her can give you some much-needed release. And when you see her get up again and line up for the next race, she is a good model for you.

Hormones, or whatever the trigger is for this increase of emotion, make feelings seem to come from nowhere, but they are just an exaggeration of what you already feel. And having highly attuned feelings will help you be more responsive to your own needs and your baby's too.

Loneliness

The baby might not be the only one plagued with loneliness. Although you've had nine months to get used to the idea, becoming a parent happens overnight. And as your old life fades into the background and your new one has yet to get itself established, becoming lonely is a real danger. Unless you are in the centre of a large family or other group who are geographically and emotionally close to you, it is usual to feel lonely as a new parent.

Juli is a thirty-two-year-old mother of one. Johann, the baby's father, left her when the baby was two months old. Juli told me, 'I didn't sign up to do this alone, but as soon as Sophie came along he left.' She was shocked, panicky – and lonely. Loneliness is a feeling that afflicts many parents, even if they haven't just been left by their partner. What made Juli feel even more lonely was that her parents seemed not to be able to see, or to admit, how near to her wits' end she was.

Loneliness used to be associated with poor social skills or being a bit odd, so there's still stigma and shame attached to it. But there shouldn't be: loneliness affects everyone. It's felt so strongly because it's alerting you to what you need to do – find company. Humans are not isolates; we are pack animals. We feel hungry when we need to eat, we feel physical pain when we need to get out of the fire, and we feel lonely when we need to be with other people and feel seen and accepted by them. Loneliness is a necessary feeling, just like thirst and hunger. Ignore it at your peril, as it can be a major cause of deterioration of mental and physical health.

When we're lonely we can feel how bad it is for us, so why don't we just join a group or make more friends? Sadly, it's often not that easy. Juli was exhausted and having to do something about her loneliness felt like another job she had no energy for. But there's another reason why tackling loneliness feels so hard. Feelings of loneliness trigger a state of hyper-vigilance for social threat and rejection, make us super-sensitive to possible rejection or coolness. And when we expect social threat, we can behave in ways that are more likely to get us rejected. Even though we may feel on the edge, we fear putting ourselves back into the centre again in case we are rebuffed – and therefore we pull ourselves even further away from people. This is how expecting to be rejected can become a self-fulfilling prophecy.

Juli's confidence took a nosedive after her partner left and she began to think of herself as 'useless'. The thought of joining a parents' support group or going to the mother-and-baby singing sessions she saw advertised locally made her just want to curl up indoors and never come out. It's not only humans that feel like this; separate any social creature from their group and they will feel wary of rejoining that group or wary of joining a new group, in case they are pushed away and find themselves even more isolated. Research has shown that rats, and even fruit flies, after they've been separated from their group, don't throw themselves back into the middle of it but stay on the edges. We have an advantage over rats and fruit flies: we can use reasoning to override our instincts to get what we need. Yet it feels hard and we come up with all sorts of excuses not to do it. It is normal to feel that you won't fit into a new group and to make up reasons for that, the most common of which are thinking that you are somehow inferior ('They'll all know what they're doing and I don't') or superior ('I don't want to join a group of parents who will only want to talk about weaning and nappies'). It may seem surprising that Juli, who a few months before had been a competent HR professional, couldn't face joining a group, but it isn't. People in isolation are more likely to scorn the idea of social interaction by thinking they are somehow better, or somehow worse, than other people, and thus give themselves an excuse not to try. Both these thought patterns – 'I'm too good' and 'I'm not good enough' – lead to a spiral of withdrawal and intensify the sense of social isolation.

It felt like a big step for Juli to admit the loneliness and talk herself into joining a group to combat it.

> I've joined a breastfeeding-support group that I found through Facebook and it's made a world of difference. We meet up a couple of afternoons a week in each other's houses. It's good to have other mums listen to my experience, and I feel useful when I can offer support to them too. The group is online as well, which is invaluable in the middle of the night – so many of us are awake anyway! I can see I got into a habit of telling myself I was useless. Sharing with other parents about this and other woes has not made them go away but it has made them more manageable.

Exercise for coping with loneliness

1. Be prepared to recognize when you are lonely. Don't deny it or judge yourself negatively for feeling it.
2. Understand what loneliness does to you: remember, as a member of a social species, it's dangerous to feel isolated.
3. Learn to recognize that hyper-vigilant state so you can override it – don't be a fruit fly. Quite often, new parents don't want to join groups because they'll feel too clever for them or too inadequate, so watch out for such feelings of superiority or inferiority. They're just excuses to cling to the distrust that loneliness can produce.

4. Reach out and be reachable. See what parent and baby groups are available near you, see if you can connect with other local parents online, ask friends over to visit and visit friends.

Post-natal depression

Loneliness can be a factor in post-natal depression too, although depression after the birth or the acquisition of parental responsibility has many causes. Symptoms of post-natal depression include: irritability, deep sadness and despair, feeling useless, anxiety, insomnia, every small thing feeling like it takes a huge effort, wanting to hide away from others, thoughts of self-harm and, in extreme cases, psychosis. Post-partum depression affects 10 to 15 per cent of new mothers each year. Several studies also suggest that as many as 10 per cent of fathers also suffer from this psychological disorder.

This is Paula's experience of post-natal depression:

> Ricky screamed when I didn't pick him up and he screamed when I did. When I handed him to my partner, she seemed to know what to do more than me. I began to feel I didn't know what I was doing. I was terrified I would somehow break Ricky doing a nappy change. I was so ashamed about how I felt I told anyone who asked, including my health visitor, that I was 'fine'.
>
> I was sure there must be something wrong with Ricky, though, to cry so much. I took him to the GP's surgery, but they could find nothing wrong. I felt even worse because then I felt ashamed for taking him in.
>
> I began to feel my baby would be better off without me. I couldn't even breastfeed as my nipples hurt so much – it felt like pins going through me. Bottle-feeding made me feel like even more of a failure.

It all came to a head when Ricky was twelve weeks old. I completely broke down and my partner and my brother saw I wasn't coping. They wouldn't accept my reply of 'fine' any longer. I had to confess I wanted to die, or at least run away. I have never felt so awful, so bleak, so depressed. It felt much bigger than just becoming a mother. A dense cloud of misery had descended on me.

It was tough on my partner because she had to do most of the baby care. She was finding it hard to cope too, although she wasn't in the dark place I was, and I don't think she had time for my feelings as well as everything else. She made me go to therapy, which made me angry at the time because it felt like she was pushing me away. I thought she and the baby were the couple and I was being pushed out.

When I look back at this period it seems unreal as I was, in a matter-of-fact way, planning to kill myself. I believed everyone would be better off without me. I fully expected to follow it through – but thought I'd try therapy first.

The therapist asked me to think about my own babyhood. I couldn't remember it so I asked my family. My cousin told me that when I was three months old my parents had handed me into the care of an aunt and a nanny and gone abroad for a month without me. I asked them why they'd done this. My father said they were getting a bit fed up with being in the world of baby and needed a break. My mum told me she was so upset when they came back because I didn't recognize her. And she said it in a tone as though she was still cross with me.

I felt sad because I hadn't been enough for her as a baby, and anger that she had left me. And I realized why Ricky felt like an alien to me – I had felt like an alien to my own mother. I realized why I felt my partner and Ricky were the couple and I was pushed out, because as a baby I really had been pushed out. I started to think, 'No wonder I felt I couldn't do it, my parents couldn't do it either.'

Making this connection somehow helped. I began slowly, indiscernibly, to get better. When Ricky was eight months old, I realized I was his mother and therefore I had to be there for him. I came to a sort of acceptance that I was for him and he was for me. I could connect more with him and feel for Ricky when he cried rather than take it as though it was a punishment directed at me.

After a year of going to therapy weekly I was not back to my normal self but I was more accepting of my new normal self. Gradually, I got to know this new version of myself – and even got to like her. And, by the way, my son is a kind and lovely twenty-two-year-old now.

It can help to find a narrative that makes sense of your feelings, like Paula did. Even knowing there is a narrative that would make sense of how you feel, even if you do not know what it is, can be sufficient.

The more we can speak about impulses and reactions we have in relation to our baby and have them understood and accepted, the more we are able to reflect and to perceive the baby as a baby and not as an object on to which we are unknowingly projecting a monster or a ghost from our past. And the more we can speak, the more we can feel that we are not a monster because we imagine we may harm the baby or fantasize about escaping from them or running away from our life. Remember: a fantasy is not harmful when it is just a fantasy. Talking about fantasies and feelings can help to place them where they were first felt, that is, to think about them in the context of our own upbringing. This can help to minimize them.

I believe we all need someone non-judgemental to talk to, someone we can be fully and unapologetically ourselves with – that is how your baby needs to use you, after all. This person or people can be other parents who understand. Or, if you want to speak to a therapist or your doctor, do not hesitate because you're thinking you don't feel bad enough to warrant it or so bad they will be shocked and horrified. Having a baby is a big deal emotionally and physically. All the different hormones are exaggerating your emotions and, if your feelings cause you to withdraw from interacting with your baby or your family, it's a good idea to seek support and professional help.

This is Gretchen's experience of post-natal depression:

> I was the first of my friendship group to have a baby. I missed my old life. I missed work and I missed seeing people. At work, I was a high achiever with high standards. As a mother, I felt as if I was wrong all the time. I did all the right things, like going to mother-and-baby groups, but when I was there I'd compare myself with the other mothers and find myself lacking.
>
> When my baby cried it grated on me rather than making me want to soothe him. Leaving the house was so stressful I thought I'd end up forgetting the baby in a shop, so most of the time I didn't bother. I avoided answering the door. Even getting dressed was too much some days. I wasn't sleeping much. I'd needed forceps at the delivery and I'd found the whole procedure very invasive. When I did get to sleep I'd keep waking up, reliving the whole nightmarish experience of the birth.
>
> Just before my boyfriend got home I'd get dressed. I'd tell him everything was wonderful. I thought if I told him or anyone just how useless I felt they would judge me. He did notice I was nervous and shaky and kept asking me what was wrong. I said it was just lack of sleep and I was okay. I really wasn't okay.
>
> I dragged myself to another local mother-and-baby group, ready to pretend I was fine again, just so I'd have something to tell my boyfriend when he got home. One woman there, Suzi, announced that she was not coping, described how awful she felt. The others started to give her advice, which I could see just made her feel worse. I took my courage in both hands and said, 'Me too,' and I told her my experience. We became

friends. Suzi found out about a group for women with depression – together, we thought this is what we had. The group had a crèche. All we mums did was crafts – like kids, sticking bits of cloth on to paper to make collages – but it was the best thing for both of us. As we stuck and sewed things, everyone just talked. Told it like it was. I think realizing I wasn't a freak and other people were going through the same thing was what made the depression begin to shift.

Three years later, I have a great relationship with my son. Our sticky start doesn't seem to have done much damage. I now have a second child, a daughter who was born a year ago. The differences this time are that now I'm not isolated and I don't believe that, unless everything is perfect, I'm a failure. It's not that I think these are the reasons for my depression after my son was born, it just felt hormonal to me.

Remember: your experience and your feelings after a baby comes into your life are not right and they are not wrong. However weird and unusual they seem to you, do not keep them to yourself. Find like-minded people to talk to like Gretchen did, and don't hesitate to seek professional help. Don't think you are not in a bad enough state, or in too bad a state, to do this. You not only owe it to yourself to feel present and correct, you owe it to your child.

Exercise: The hidden parts of parenting

The following exercise is what is called a guided visualization. You will be asked to visualize a scenario in your mind's eye and the idea is to really explore it to try to find out what's going on in your hidden depths.

Imagine three rooms. The first one is a reception room, then two doors lead off the reception room into the second room and the third room. Think of this three-roomed house as a metaphor for you as a parent. In your mind's eye, go to the reception room.

This is where you receive visitors. Here, you have your public face on.

The second room is where you feel most unsure, and perhaps most angry, regretful, ashamed, frustrated, sad or dissatisfied. This is the room of difficulty and vulnerability when it comes to being a parent. Walk into that room and dare to feel what it feels like in here. Have a look round and note what you see without judging yourself. As you spend time in this room and feel what it is like to be in here, notice your breathing. If you were holding your breath or breathing shallowly, breathe normally again. Take one last look round the room of difficulty and then come back into the reception room again, back into the public space. Notice what it feels like to shut the door on the room of difficulty but know that the difficulty is still there.

Now it's time to open the door to the third room. This is the room where you feel most positive. In this room everything is going right, you feel a sense of pride in who you are as a parent and you feel the joy you can feel with your child or children, and possibly more pride than you could show in the reception room. Have a look round the positive room and see what it is that is there. Keep looking and notice what you feel in this room. Good.

Now come back into the reception room. As you stand in the reception room, have a good sense of what is behind both closed doors. Remember: we all have these rooms as well as the public face of parenting when other people can see us with our children. And we all have how we feel about ourselves as parents, things we feel great about and things we feel less than great about. What is so important is not to compare our own private room of difficult feelings to other people's public face of parenting.

Remember: we all need someone accepting to talk to about those two rooms off the reception room. Someone who can hear us when we feel flooded with love and someone who can accept us and the more ambiguous feelings that parenting brings up.

PART FIVE

Conditions for Good Mental Health

It's fantastic that our society is finally talking about children's mental health and what we can do to bolster it. But it's sad that children's mental health is at crisis point. In this section I will refer to the early weeks and months and the early years a lot, as they are so important when it comes to instilling a sense of security in our children, but, as I keep emphasizing, it is never too late to take steps to attempt to repair any rupture that may have happened during the early years if your child is older.

There are no guarantees that a deprived, terrible childhood will result in mental-health problems later, or that an ideal childhood will protect someone from losing their mind. Having said that, there are things we can do that will give your children the best possible chance to minimize any potential mental-health problems. We owe it to them and to ourselves to take a course that has the greatest likelihood of resulting in a healthy mind and body.

The bond

One of the most important indicators for good mental health is a strong bond between parent and child.

Humans are pack animals; we have lived in tribes for millennia. We are wired to bond to each other; it is how we survive as a species. The most primary bond of all is that of child and parent, parent and child. You will have a bond with your child and your child is hard-wired to form one with you. But how can you make that bond as rewarding as possible for both of you, and one that is most likely to create a capacity for health and happiness? I've talked about how important it is to keep a baby company, to be alongside them as they experience their feelings and moods so they don't feel alone. I've also talked about how important it is for a baby to be physically close to their parents. But how, in addition to being physically close, do we get emotionally close to a baby or a young child? After all, it's not as though you can both use words. What creates your bond and your relationship is give and take. By that, I am talking about the mutual influence we have on each other. It might seem obvious that I affect you, you affect me and we form a unique relationship together, different from other relationships we have with other people. And this is what will probably unconsciously happen, or has already happened, between you and your baby. I am starting with infants because that's when the parenting relationship begins, but what I have to say about to-and-fro communication, about the desirability of dialogue being like a collaborative dance, is relevant to any relationship.

The give and take, to and fro of communication

Initially, when your baby makes a noise, they are communicating with you. A baby's noises, their gestures, their coercive cries and the way they initiate turn-taking games are the forerunner to conversation. With all of these, your child is looking for your reciprocity.

If you tell them to 'shush', you are telling them that their communication is not welcome. Over time and many 'shushes', this may make them feel that they are not welcome. I am no fan of the 'shush'. I see nothing wrong with a pacifier when used in conjunction with attention and loving touch to help soothe a child, but I don't like it being used as a stopper, to gag the essential to and fro of communication.

Before our children learn to articulate their feelings we learn their cues by observing them. They may be minutes or years old, but they will have their unique viewpoint of the world. I believe the happiest parents are those who are open and willing to learn from their children, to keep expanding their viewpoint by taking in their children's. A child whose person and point of view is respected learns innately to respect others. They can take it for granted that there is more than one way of seeing things and experiencing things.

If you are parents to a baby and you just want to gaze at your baby and have 'conversations' with them made up of gestures and facial expressions, this is exactly what you need to do. This 'game' is what develops into the give and take of dialogue. And it helps to strengthen your bond, as it develops your relationship. Later on, we lose sight of our body-to-body communications with our children as words gradually take over, but it will still be there. It is still relevant to observe a child as well as hear them in order to fully listen to them and to allow them to impact on you. And indeed, this is relevant to adult relationships as well.

In a dialogue, whether it's just looks and gestures or includes sounds or speech, both parties affect each other. When I say 'gestures', I am talking about all body movements, some deliberate and some more like body-to-body communication as we pick up on each other's moods and intentions. It's not one partner being all teacher and giver and the other all recipient and sponge. It's not just one body affecting the other body but both bodies affecting each other. This is how a fulfilling relationship develops. Mutual impact is key to all our relationships – and that's true for a child-and-parent pairing too. Too often it is easy to be in too much of a rush, and then a relationship, instead of being in a steady rhythm of to and fro and turn-taking, becomes instead about being what I call 'Doing and Done to', where one party is dominant and the other submissive rather than each being an equal partner in the communication exchange. This happens when we do not leave a gap for the other to respond and, if this becomes a habit, the relationship can lose its way.

Think of it like a teacher with a class. The teachers who engage their pupils are the ones who read a class and tailor their teaching to that class. They are not afraid to learn from the pupils in turn. They find out what the pupils know already, they keep them interested by getting them to brainstorm, they check they've been understood before putting the next piece of information in place. A classroom working like this is a peaceful place of to and fro, whereas when a teacher just gives out information to the pupils, they are likely to become resentful or restless and don't learn as much.

Where we feel most frustrated and find relationships to be the most unsatisfactory is when we do not have an impact. It doesn't matter what we say and do, the person or organization does not heed us, even if they are doing things to us, and we can begin to feel hopeless, isolated or rebellious. So it is important to allow yourself to be impacted by your children – let them influence you. You will be modelling how to be influenced, which is important so that your children in turn allow themselves to be influenced by you.

How dialogue begins

An example of very early dialogue is breathing together. A baby's breathing is automatic. However, with time, a baby learns that breathing can also be controlled voluntarily and that they can regulate their breathing. They may automatically tune in to the breathing of the adult they're being held by or lying in contact with. The synchronization of breathing may be part of how we bond. I found lying by my baby and synchronizing my breathing to hers and noticing when she synched to mine both rewarding and moving. Perhaps this is why we sing to and with children, be it nursery rhymes or pop music, because to sing together is to both breathe and play together.

Breathing exercise

Face your partner or a friend and take it in turns to follow each other's patterns of breathing. Notice how you feel when you follow, how you feel when you lead, and do this until you relax into the exercise. Give it a while, or at least until you do notice what feelings you are having in reaction to this exercise.

Turn-taking

Another type of interaction you may have with a very young baby may be in the form of a game of looking at each other, then looking away, taking it in turns to initiate the game. This type of game has a uniqueness because you invent it together. During the game, the baby may turn away with a blank expression and, instead of turning back, stay looking away. The parent, in response, sits back and waits for the baby to make their next move. Then the baby looks at them once more with a curious and smiley expression. The parent may say, in a gentle, high-pitched voice, 'Oh, hello again, you've come back!' Then the baby may repeat the process many times until they feel satisfied.

When mothers and their four-month-old infants show patterns of turn-taking between give and take, watching, listening and responding, researchers can predict that, when the infant is a year old, Mum and baby will have a secure attachment bond. If we think about the desert metaphor, this is the baby feeling rescued from the desert and made to feel welcome. They can take for granted that their needs, including their relational needs, will be, more often than not, met.

Of course, like all things human, bonding can go wrong. As a parent, you can interrupt and interfere with the natural process by not observing, not listening, not seeing the world sufficiently from the child's standpoint. So, if a parent 'misses' too many cues from the baby, or is too demanding of the baby, it's unlikely the baby will learn to feel secure in this main relationship – that is, until the parent changes their pattern of relating by becoming observant and responsive.

You may find this kind of attuned reciprocity draining and demanding rather than natural and effortless. This is not your fault. It might be to do with how you were initially responded to when you were a baby, or you may not naturally attune to other people or only with difficulty.

When dialogue is difficult: diaphobia

Personally, I did not find reciprocity an easy thing to do. I had to work at it. Maybe this was because being listened to and considered was not an everyday experience for me as I was growing up. It may be that you have an unconscious rule or a belief that one person (the adult) should always be the doer and the other (the child) the done to. In that case, reciprocity gets stuck.

Do you naturally and easily let your child affect you as you adapt to one another and find listening and responding to your children natural, automatic and easy? Not everyone has this natural response readily available – some of us must work to recover it within us. Maybe you notice some resistance to letting your child, be they a baby, a toddler or even an adult, affect you. This is called diaphobia, a phobia of real dialogue, of being impacted upon by others, a fear of being 'done to'.

We tend to do what has been done to us when we were babies and children. And it can be as though our natural innate ability to respond has been deadened. It may be that you were well cared for in practical terms but you did not experience reciprocity in your own infancy. If your feelings were not taken seriously, if you were thought of as less than human and more of an 'it', if you were seen only as 'the baby', 'the child' or one of 'the children' rather than as an individual, if you were not allowed to affect your adults, you may well have some diaphobia.

For babies and children, being responded to is a need, not a want. If we don't respond to a child's cries, glances or turn-taking games, if we don't play our part in the give and take they offer us, there's a danger of fostering in them insecure or avoidant attachment styles and personality traits. This will make it much harder for them to have functional relationships.

However, if you feel you may be diaphobic, do not admonish yourself, blame yourself or feel ashamed. Now you know what you are doing to interrupt the give and take, you can make the changes that enable you to attune to your child. Be proud that you have detected it and faced up to it. It can sometimes be easier to spot diaphobia in others than it is to see it in ourselves. But try to notice when you are shying away from the contact of give and take with your baby or child, teenager or adult child. Notice if you tend to talk at them, rather than with them. Learn to give in to that instinct and give your child the sort of give-and-take attention they need.

You may be reading this while having regretful pangs: 'It's too late, I've already been diaphobic with my child.' Don't. You have a bond with your child and you can always work on making it better. You can start listening, you can start to see the world from their perspective as well as your own, you can allow them to be different from you and you can allow their influence on you. It means a great deal even to adult children when their parents can see them as equals and take on board what their children show and tell them. Of course, you can repair the rupture before they are adults. If you realize that you have been batting your child away, you can stop. I'm not saying that you should completely surrender your standpoint, all your opinions and defer only to the child's – not at all. What I am saying is that their way of seeing the world is as equally valid as yours.

Let's hear from John, aged forty-two.

My partner recently asked, 'Why can't you bear to be told anything?' It quite shook me. It got me thinking and I realized I have a real shame of not knowing things. She also told me that my catchphrase could be 'I know.' I pepper all my sentences with it, apparently, whether I do know or not.

Then I visited my father. He was getting in a muddle with his medication so I drew up a chart for him – what he should be taking and when. And he said, sarcastically, 'You think I've lived eighty-six years on this earth by not knowing how to read the labels on these pill bottles, do you?' I realized that he too hated being told something he might not know.

If I'm honest, I can see that Dad's long-standing you-can't-tell-me-anything attitude has always been and still is hurtful to me. A more appropriate response from him would have been, 'Thank you for doing that, I was getting in a muddle,' but he could not bear to be told, and especially not by his son. I may be over forty but I am, to him, still a boy.

Then I realized I never really listen to my own son, as I don't consider he may have something to tell me that I don't know. I noticed he was developing the 'I know' habit from me.

My partner has been helping me to be more open and to listen more and not to feel ashamed when I don't know. I now let my son show me things too, and not in a patronizing way, and it is really improving our relationship. I didn't use to leave the space. It was as though I thought the communication should be one way only, from me to him, from the teacher to the pupil, but now I'm learning to leave space for him to show me who he is. And I'm learning to find out who he is rather than assuming I know.

I was the classic man cliché, not wanting to ask for directions because I couldn't bear to be told something I didn't know by someone else. So now I'm asking everyone for directions all the time, letting myself feel that shame of not knowing things. But I'm not acting on the shame, I'm not allowing it to crush my curiosity any more or stop me listening to my boy like it used to. And it isn't destroying me, quite the opposite. In the short space of time since I have been aware of this, I already feel so much closer to him.

Sometimes, making a change, such as deciding not to give in to diaphobia, which is what John decided to do, even though he did not have the word for it, feels like it will have terrible consequences, but it turns out this small change in behaviour brings forth a lot of benefits.

Exercise: Notice your behaviour patterns

If, when your child wants some attention, you nearly always think of something that's more urgent, such as doing chores or work or making a call, and you use this as an excuse to yourself and to them to push them away, this is probably your diaphobia in action. Notice when you are doing this. Stop, override the instinct to push them away and instead engage and include them in whatever task it is you have to do.

Exercise: Can you be told things?

What does it feel like to be told something you already know? What does it feel like to be told something you feel you should know but don't? Try not to answer these questions with what you think you should say but with what you really feel when this happens. Whatever feeling is brought up for you doing the exercise, can you trace its origins in your childhood?

You don't have to be in constant, 24/7, face-to-face action and reaction with your child. But what the research shows is that when you are with your child and you ignore most of their bids for attention it is distressing for them. In one experiment, mothers were instructed to sit with their baby face to face but not to show any mimicking or gesturing in response to the baby – that is, not to show any emotional responsiveness. After the mothers did that for only three minutes, the babies reacted with distress. They showed anxiety, shame and sadness that lingered for several minutes. You can think of it as the baby being left to dance on their own.

Children need reciprocity from their caregivers; otherwise, they learn helplessness, that their actions have no effect. If a baby could put their experience into words they may think, 'If I cannot affect you, then I do not exist.' This is why some infants seem to give up. By not responding to enough of our infant's cues, we accidentally teach them not to try.

The importance of engaged observation

Quite often, when we think we are listening, all we are doing is waiting for a gap for an opportunity to speak back; we use our energy to compose our response or our reply rather than to try to understand what the other person is trying to communicate. Stopping doing this, and allowing instead the other person to impact upon us, can feel scary. It doesn't feel scary if we put this fear into words, but it does when we have an unspoken fear that, if we really listen and allow ourselves to be impacted, we ourselves will disappear. We will not disappear – quite the opposite, we will grow. This is Jodie and Jo's story.

> In our first few weeks together I often felt drained by the neediness of my baby, Jo. I wanted to be open to her, to respond to her cries, but it was a struggle. It felt as if giving in to her demands would mean losing myself, that I'd be taken over by her.
>
> What helped me become more open towards Jo, rather than trying to defend myself against her demands, was watching her. When I was with her, giving her my attention, she'd call

on me less. I slowly got the knack of pre-empting some of her crying by learning to read her cues before she got distressed.

I began to talk to Jo with a running commentary as I did any housework or tasks, leaving spaces for her to 'chat' back at me. When I didn't need to do anything, instead of playing with my phone or picking up a book, I would pay her attention.

I realized that, instead of always trying to show her stuff, if I looked at what she was looking at too, let her show me what she liked, it was more rewarding. She would look at things and I'd bring them closer to her or take her to them and look at them with her. She taught me to stop and to look, because I'd forgotten how to do that. It's not that I got a thrill from examining a leaf or a ladybird, or watching SpongeBob Square-Pants, but watching her concentrate on things filled me with something; perhaps you'd call it awe, or even just love.

As Jo got older and started to talk I noticed my relationship with her was always better when I listened. Sometimes, I'd forget and talk at her or over her. And then she'd be less responsive – and I'd realize I'd fallen back into an old way of communicating, one that didn't work for either of us.

Leaving space for Jo has mellowed me, made me feel more loving, not only to her but to other people and things. Jo is nearly grown up now and I think I'm more of a grown-up than I was because I expanded my own view so much from watching her, listening to her, seeing things from her perspective. Talking now about how she affects me fills me with love. Love that maybe I was incapable of before I was a parent. I feel expanded by her.

Jodie's experience is about her relationship with her baby, about a new pattern of being with and responding she learned in relationship to her child. By really listening, rather than just thinking about her response or only about what she wanted to impart, she formed a deep loving and liking relationship with Jo.

We can all do this, with our babies, children, adult children and, indeed, with anyone.

What happens when you're addicted to your phone

If you're physically close to your child but are missing their cues because, say, you are on your phone or computer, it will trouble them. Think how you feel when you go out with a friend and they spend too much of your time together on their phone. Annoying, right? Because you have, more or less, already formed your personality, it isn't going to damage you, although it won't help the relationship. Your child, however, is in the process of forming their personality and their habits in relationship with you.

We know that alcoholics and drug addicts do not make the best parents because their priority is always the substance they're addicted to, so their children are denied a lot of the attention they need. I'd say phone addicts are not so far behind. I do not recommend playing or checking emails on your phone in front of a young child for long periods of time. Not only will you be depriving them of contact, you will be creating an empty space inside them. And not to be dramatic, but this is the sort of empty space that may make addicts of people later in life, when they try to fill it with addictive substances or compulsive activities to stop a feeling of being disconnected – feeling empty – haunting them.

You also risk your child becoming addicted to a screen too, as a replacement for contact. You may get more of an instant sense of connection from a screen than from meaningful contact with another person – but it is not a viable substitute.

You may well be attached to your phone because of your need for contact. Well, your child has the same need for contact, but more intensely, because they need contact with you to connect up their brain. People do not develop normally in isolation. People need people.

Anyone who cares for your baby or child needs to know this about screens too, whether it's a nanny, a childminder, a friend or a relative. If you or they are always staring at a screen, your child will want a screen to stare at too. If you have suddenly realized on reading this that you often ignore your child, do not think, 'I have ruined them for life,' because you haven't. Simply by stopping and making the space for them instead, you can repair your relationship.

We are born with an innate capacity for dialogue

There was another observation from the maternal-response experiment, and that was how difficult it was for many mothers to maintain a still face when looking at their baby. This shows how powerful the infant's signals are, how we're wired to respond. We just need to let it happen.

We are born with this innate capacity for dialogue, to interact, to take turns. This process begins from birth and it does not stop. Maybe it starts before that; maybe the birth process is a form of turn-taking too, contraction followed by rest?

In dialogue, one person's action produces a turn-taking response in the other. In the turn-taking the parent and the baby meet with their own different rhythms. Both tune in and learn from each other. Together, infants and their parents develop unique patterns of being together. A baby and one parent may develop one pattern and the same baby and their other parent may develop another, a baby and a sibling another, and so on. Each relationship has a different pattern.

These patterns are not adult led but co-created between the baby and the other person. They are not all fixed – they change depending on the moods and the input of each partner. Sometimes the partners 'get' each other and sometimes they miss, then some readjustment needs to take place.

The way you'll find out what your child wants is by observing, by trial, by repairing former misses by trying again and succeeding. You may learn to read a certain glance as 'I am ready for more smiling'; and at another time you may learn that a similar glance means 'Feed me.' It is very normal not to be able to understand what a baby means with their cries or gestures, and that's okay, but you can still respond in your own way. It isn't the sense that matters so much as the pattern of turn-taking. I felt inadequate as a new mother when more experienced parents told me I would be able to interpret the cries before too long and that one would mean the baby is thirsty and another that the baby is too hot. Cries to me were not inadequate language, they were sounds, communications of a different sort, requiring my attention and observation and engagement but not a non-existent baby-dictionary. It felt easier once patterns of observing and turn-taking were established.

A baby learns to communicate and find connection by being with their family, and members of that family learn by being with that baby, as each pairing develops their unique communications system. It's like the way in which the best stand-up comics read a room and adapt to it to give their performance. No two audiences and no two babies are the same. After a few months each partner knows each other better and has learned how to be with each other in ways they can each find more satisfying; observing and turn-taking has a major part to play in this, even though, for the most part, it is done unconsciously.

This is Simon's story:

> By watching my son, Ned, I realized he was communicating right from the off. I didn't always understand what he was telling me, but watching him helped me get there. I got to know the signs I needed to do something about and the ones that weren't so urgent.
>
> Ned has just turned two and he can say quite a few words and use short sentences. But he still doesn't always know what he needs – so we still have to watch him to get that.

Last weekend, we were at a restaurant with another family who have bigger kids and Ned was loving chatting to them and playing. Then I noticed his eyes glaze over, and he'd stopped looking at them. We have learned this is what Ned does when he's had enough of something, needs a bit of quiet time. If we don't notice it, what happens next is he can start crying, even go into full tantrum mode.

This time, I spotted it, so I got up and asked Ned if he wanted to go for a walk, and he nodded. I picked him up from his high chair and carried him out of the restaurant. We sat on the grass outside and he leaned against me for a minute or two. Then he started to pick daisies and give them to me. We began a familiar game where I count whatever it is he's handing me: one daisy, two daisies, three daisies. Then he takes them back, to hand them to me again.

I could see Ned was calm and engaged once more and had lost that spaced-out look. When he'd finished with the daisies, he was looking around for something else to take his attention, and I said, 'Shall we go back inside and finish the meal?' He nodded, took my hand and led me back to the table.

What surprises me is that it wasn't a pain to have to leave a group of friends because I feel so engaged with Ned. He has taught me to communicate more on a bodily level, by watching him and learning what his triggers and needs are.

When a baby has a low impact on their parents – isn't 'demanding', is 'easy' or 'good' – it is often, in some childcare philosophies, considered a good thing. But manipulating a baby into having the least effect on you is dehumanizing. You need to allow your baby to impact you. If you don't, the child will have to overadapt to feel like they belong and in so doing they lose a sense of themselves and some of their humanity (like we may have lost some of our own when we were babies). Babies may not yet know words, but we can learn to understand them by observing them.

If we practise this skill of observation, it will help us to understand and relate better to our children, whatever age they are.

Babies and children are people too

As adults, we know it's respectful to be mindful of any person that we come into contact with. But sometimes people forget that babies are people too. Try to think of your child as a partner in the enterprise of being cared for.

This is why it matters to get into the habit of telling your child what is going to happen, then leaving a pause before making something happen. So, for example, suppose your baby is in a pushchair and you're going to lift them out and put them in a car seat. Say, 'I'm going to lift you into the car seat,' then leave a pause so they can take it in. Then tell them what's happening, as it happens: 'Now I'm unbuckling you. I'm going to lift you out and put you in the car seat.' You may feel awkward because the child might not have language yet, but we learn language by hearing it. What is more important than the words is the to and fro between you and your child, the turn-taking.

Over time, when they get used to this, as the give and take of dialogue beds in and you leave spaces for them to respond, they will put out their arms to help you lift them. Do the same when you are going to change their nappy or their clothes. Involve them in as many of your activities as you can, but especially those that are to do with them.

People develop in relationship with each other. The more open we are to the other and the more sensitive we can be to the subtleties of glance and gesture, agitation or relaxation, the more we can ward off unhappiness and despair in our babies and therefore in ourselves. We can learn to relax and to observe our babies and children, to respect their individual activities and communications and learn from them. It makes parenting, which, as you know, can feel long and boring in the early months and years, seem less so, because it gives it meaning.

Positive attention given to your child is never wasted. I think we can sometimes err in thinking it's the grand gestures that matter – the trip to a theme park, the big Christmas present, the birthday party. These things can be nice but it is the everyday interactions that count. With trial and error on both sides, the minutiae of everyday interaction will become as satisfying as possible to both of you and give your young human a capacity for happiness.

Exercise: How to get better at dialogue

To get even better at dialogue, think about how you listen and observe when you are listening well – to your baby, to another child or to an adult. You'll realize that what happens is you notice the movements, tone, gestures and expressions of the speaker, you concentrate on what is being said and you may be aware of the feelings the speaker brings up in you.

So what can get in the way of your listening and observing? Often, it's prematurely preparing your response in your head, or your mind otherwise wandering off. Of course, these things will always happen to some extent, but what you can do is notice when you've stopped focusing on the speaker or the child or baby – and return your attention to them. With practice, you'll get better at being a good listener and being an equal partner in this dialogue.

How we train our children to be annoying – and how to break that cycle

While doing some research for a TV programme I made about surrealism, I learned that when Salvador Dalí was at school he once charged headfirst into a marble pillar, hurting himself quite badly. When asked why he'd done that, he said it was because no one was paying him any attention.

If babies and children don't get what they need at the beginning of their lives, if they don't feel seen, if they can't be certain they will be responded to, they may get locked into the stage of trying to get attention. And that's when you – and other people – might experience them as annoying.

I can put this another way: you can't 'spoil' a baby with too much sensitive responsiveness to their cues. Time invested in the beginning gets the child used to having their needs for connection met. They internalize this, know they can rely on it and don't have to keep looking for it. If they don't get enough attention, the child can get stuck in feeling real only when they have a direct behavioural or emotional impact on those around them.

A child given enough attention will feel secure, won't have to be preoccupied with relationships, neither obsessing about them nor feeling they must perform – jump through hoops or charge into pillars – to be sure of them. If you don't respond to most of a child's bids for attention, they will make those bids louder or, as they get older, naughtier. Negative attention from a parent is better than no attention at all because at least then they know they exist in your mind. They feel compelled to be disruptive, which, of course, ostracizes them further.

Once a child is a pain, they are harder to get along with and to pay attention to, which is a shame, because they need attention even more, to repair the early rupture.

What if your relationship with your child feels as if you're both locked into some sort of battle where all the attention seems to be negative attention and you experience them as an irritation? First, you might want to find somewhere else, away from your child and home, to safely release the anger that has built up in you. This might be talking to someone who won't judge you, or it may be going into a soundproof room, beating a cushion with your fists and having a good old roar.

To reverse the relationship you have, and what you have been doing, you can do what psychologist Oliver James calls 'love bombing'. James says, in order to reset the emotional thermostat of your child – and, I add, probably yours too – you need to spend some time with your child. Not 'quality time' when you just hang out together but love-bombing time. This is a time with a marked beginning and an end when your child, within reason, calls the shots. It's the child who decides what you'll do and where you'll do it.

Love bombing is one-to-one time, so make it either at home when the rest of the family are visiting relatives or, perhaps, if you can afford it, at a hotel. For the whole period – of twenty-four hours or a weekend – your child, so long as it's safe and legal, is in charge of what you both do and eat. And during that time, you also frequently express your heartfelt appreciation and love for your child.

It may feel as if, by letting your child call the shots and showering them with love, you are compounding their bad behaviour, but you are not. Imagine you felt unseen, unheard or mistreated (it does not really make any difference if you are mistaken in this – if you feel it, it is your experience) by the people whose love, good opinion and attention are your source of connection and everything that matters, and the only way you were sure of getting their attention was to make a nuisance of yourself. If they gave you that love and consideration, you would not have to play up to get attention. The love-bombing exercise gives the child a concentrated dose of that attention. It also interrupts your mutually coercive patterns of behaviour and resets both of you in a rhythm and pattern of give and take.

In my practice as a psychotherapist I have met adults who get stuck at the stage of wanting attention all the time; otherwise, they feel shame or they feel that they don't really exist. If you don't respond to most of your child's cues, you might be training them to be manipulative like this too. The other outcome is that they will give up on relationships altogether and become hard to form a connection with. There is no avoiding, no short cuts, to giving your child the attention they need.

Doing this doesn't mean telling them that they have done a 'good job' all the time or that they are the 'greatest', which isn't necessarily a good idea. It's not about judging them. What they need is the ordinary turn-taking, the to and fro of spoken or unspoken dialogue. The more of this type of attention you invest in your baby and child, the less catching up you, and they, will need to do later.

Think of it like this: there's a parent and a child on a train. A child sitting still on a long journey is liable to get bored. The parent can either play with the child, draw with them, read to them, play a game with them – or spend the time instead telling them to be quiet and sit still. It is more pleasant for both of you to play with or read to a child – spend that time in give and take – than it is to spend the time in admonishment, or enduring noise that is unpleasant for both yourself and other people in the carriage. It often happens too that when you put the time in at the beginning of a long period, such as a train journey, your child can become absorbed in an activity you initially did together, and you may be able to have some time when they don't need you to read your book or relax by doing your own thing.

Why a child becomes 'clingy'

Don't worry if your child goes through a stage of only wanting you, or only wanting your co-parent. This is, in fact, a good sign. It means the child has formed a very strong bond and that they can form strong bonds, which is helpful for their capacity for happiness.

It's natural for a child to prefer their parent and members of their own immediate family to other carers. The more secure they feel in their bond with you, the easier they will separate to form strong bonds with others – but only when they are ready. Do not be in a hurry for this to happen. The clinging, the longing and the loving of you may seem overwhelming at times, but enjoy it: it is a sign that they have formed a strong attachment to you. The more certain they become of this attachment, the less reassurance they will need of it.

I remember one mother saying to me, 'My child adores me and needs me so much. I've never had a man this keen!' This child eventually did, like other children will, learn to take his mother so much for granted that he is now keen to go for play-dates and sleepovers. The key to fostering an independent spirit is, paradoxically, allowing them to separate from you when they are ready and want to, rather than pulling away from them.

It's not that there is anything wrong with the more sensitive child who needs to keep you close. Nor is there anything wrong with a child who wants time alone. We're all different and have different needs. We all go through stages in development, but we do so at our own pace. I am not going to give you a milestone age-marker for smiling, or sitting up, or remembering a song, because it does not mean we are any less worthy if we develop at different stages and at different speeds. The way to get through any stage a child is at is to meet their relational needs at that stage so that you and they can go through it and not get stuck in it. You cannot rush it, or ignore it, or a child may get caught there. The more positive energy you invest in your child at the start, the less of your energy you will need to invest further on.

Finding meaning in childcare

Some parents struggle with the early years because they find them boring, or unstimulating. It's true there is a lot of manual labour and the intellectual or social stimulation you get from being with babies and young children is different to what you were used to at work or in your before-baby life. A way through these struggles is to allow yourself to be interested and curious about your baby, to notice where their focus is, to try to work out what they are trying to do, rather than thinking of being with your baby as boring – of your baby as something that is 'done to'. If you get stuck in the trap of feeling that they are little more than an obligation to be fed, wiped and entertained, you are limiting what meaning you could be making from caring for your child. A meaning I made was that my care, respect and attention were an investment in my daughter and in our relationship. Looking back on those early months and years from this distance, it seems they went very fast after all. It is more useful to make a meaning like that about childcare than it is to look around the mess in your home and feel you have nothing to show, no results, for your day's work. The results will come, just not at the end of every single day, like they might in other types of work. When we adopt the habit of listening and allowing our child to impact upon us, parenting does become rewarding. When you invest in helping to keep your child feeling connected and engaged with you and with any activity they do or that you do together, you are investing in their future default mood.

Your child's default mood

Most of us have normal, resting moods that we live in for most of the time, our 'usual' moods. This may surprise you a little, but the time you spend in the natural to and fro of relating with your child is an investment that will pay off in terms of the development of their usual mood. Although we may be born with a tendency to have a certain temperament, so much of how we habitually feel does develop in relationships with others, especially our parents. The more relaxed your child is, probably because they get enough attuned attention, the more their default mood is likely to be relaxed rather than anxious or angry. Like many adults, you may have had to work hard in later life to learn how to relax because, as a baby, you got used to being anxious, or lonely or otherwise unsoothed and unmet and those feelings became an habitual mood for you. I want to stress that of course it is okay for your child to feel the whole spectrum of emotions, and they will, but they need to be kept company in all their moods, from tears to smiles and fears and anger.

When people come to therapy for the first time, they often find it a powerful experience simply because being listened to has the power to soothe. Possibly some of us would not even need therapy had we been adequately listened to. Being available to observe, listen and engage with your child in a way that makes them feel safe, loved and valuable is an investment in their default mood.

Sleep

Sleep is a huge deal – not for babies and children; they'll sleep when they sleep, but for parents. It is an emotive subject. Parents get angry and defensive about their sleep strategies, especially if they think they have found a method that works for them and then someone like me comes along and says, 'It is not kind or wise to leave your baby or toddler to cry alone in the night. It's not relating to them. It's like treating them like an "it" rather than a person.' I am not saying this because I want to shame you – I really don't – but nor do I want babies, toddlers and children to be alone at night when they feel that they need you. It is no more pleasant for a child to cry themselves to sleep or feel lonely than it is for an adult. I'm not comfortable with the idea of manipulation, or 'training', as a way of relating to anyone, but especially not to children, who are forming their personalities and attachment styles in relationship with their primary care-givers. Sleep training is when you leave a baby or a toddler to cry either until they are asleep, or until they have cried for a certain amount of time and then you go into them after a few minutes but each night you gradually make those few minutes longer and longer. There are studies that say this type of condi-tioning reduces the number of minutes it takes for a baby to go to sleep. There are even studies that say conditioning a child not to cry out for you does them no harm, but there is later research that contradicts these studies, that points out the flaws in the earlier studies and finds that sleep training harms a baby's brain development.

The main take-away from sleep-training research is that sleep training does not eliminate a baby or a child's need for you; it eliminates their crying out for you, as it conditions them to give up trying.

The parental sleep obsession is easy to understand because having interrupted sleep can leave you exhausted. But I believe our preoccupation in wanting to push our children into getting to sleep, and by themselves too, as fast and as early as possible has the potential to harm our relationship with them and there-fore has the possibility to interfere with their capacity for happiness later in life. This is because babies and children do not learn to soothe themselves and regulate their emotions by being left alone but by being soothed by a carer, time and time again. As they grow up they eventually learn to internalize that sooth-ing. In other words, we learn to self-soothe by being soothed by others. And to begin with, this soothing is a twenty-four-hour job, which can be something of a jolt for new parents.

If your child associates sleep with comfort, security and com-pany, they'll feel good about going to bed and sleeping. We get into trouble with sleep when we try to push our children away from us when we want them to sleep. Then, bedtime becomes associated with loneliness and rejection.

In most of Western culture, there seems to be some sort of race to get children to be alone at night. It might be because we prioritize our fast-paced lives and what we perceive to be society's expectations of us over the necessity of following our instincts to attend to a coercive cry. Society's expectations of parents and babies can be at odds with biology. What we need to remember is that children separate from their parents naturally. When they know you're there and available, then they feel free to separate because they can take it for granted that you'll be there when they want to reconnect. We do not encourage their independence by pulling away from them; by doing that we are interfering with the separation process and protracting it, as well as interfering with the process of our children forming a secure attachment style. All mammals sleep with their young and the majority of humans are no different. In southern Europe, Asia, Africa and Central and South America, sharing a sleeping space with parents is the norm for babies until they are fully weaned and often beyond that, as in Japan. We are in the minority in the West to think it is acceptable to have babies sleeping separately from their parents.

Night-time is half a baby's life. If they get into a habit of feeling unheard and unmet and lonely at night, there is a danger that this becomes a sort of default mood for them. If a baby is crying and is being comforted by a mother, father or another familiar figure, this is tolerable stress; if a baby is left alone to cry, it is toxic stress. An excess of the hormone cortisol will be present in toxic stress and this adversely affects how the baby's brain wires up. If you are so tired that you have slept through your child's coercive crying on a few occasions, this is unlikely to have any long-lasting adverse effect on them; it is only when there is a nightly habit of ignoring the cries of a baby who is alone that there may be a rupture you will need to repair. This is done by accepting your child's feelings, not trying to condition or scold them out of them but being alongside them and feeling with them so they know they are not alone. This is what we need to do whatever age our children are.

Sleep is one of those areas, like many areas in childrearing, where the more time you invest early on, the less time you'll spend later trying to get it right. I think the best way of investing is with empathy, lying down with your child or otherwise staying with them until they're asleep. In this way, they learn to associate sleep with feeling loved, being kept company and safe.

You may have altered sleep patterns while you invest this time in keeping them company in the night, and this is normal. It usually helps if, when the baby awakes, they can smell or touch their parent, so it can help if you sleep with your baby. This also saves you from having to get up to soothe your child.

None of us sleeps through the night. A typical sleep cycle for an adult is about ninety minutes; for an infant, it is one hour. We may think we do sleep through, but in fact what we are doing is waking up, or very nearly waking up, and going straight back to sleep again. If a baby senses you close and can touch you, they are less likely to be aroused to full wakefulness.

Please don't berate yourself if you have tried sleep training. You may have had no way of knowing that your silent child could still be stressed before you heard that the stress hormones remain high even though they have given up crying. It may well be that a lot of children can survive sleep training unscathed – individual children have different needs and different sensitivities – but personally I would never take that risk. Please don't throw this book away in a temper. I don't want you to feel ashamed if you have resorted to trying to condition your child to sleep by ignoring or delaying your response to their cries. There is so much societal pressure to force children to be alone and silent at night, it's no wonder we capitulate to it. I will be coming to alternatives. Sleep training is conditioning, it is not relating; it is treating your baby as an 'it' rather than as an individual person, it is trying to manipulate your child into having a silent night rather than allowing them to separate from you at their own pace according to their own needs.

Not many of us have pre-verbal memories, so we cannot recollect what it felt like to be left alone to go to sleep when we felt needy and lonely – and so we may not see the harm in perpetuating it. I believe, as well as developing a habit of feeling despair, what sleep training may also perpetuate is a shutting down of that feeling of despair, which also shuts down the capacity for being able to empathize with others in their distress. There's a possibility that sleep training, as well as conditioning a baby not to cry out in the night, could also contribute to feelings of shame around needing another person.

At first, a baby will cry every day, and it may seem like every hour of every day and night; a toddler will cry every day; and then, almost imperceptibly, they will cry less and less. As you comfort them, they learn how to cope with their feelings. If you ignore their cries, they will learn not to share their feelings with you – which will not help them cope with them. Having feelings accepted and soothed is the foundation for good mental health.

I know – this is all very well. Here I am, lobbing facts and opinions at you without mercy and apparently not noticing how exhausted you are. Sorry. But there are good alternatives to sleep training. There is co-sleeping, where you do not separate at night so the baby does not feel abandoned and alone. But not everyone is able or wants to sleep alongside a baby. An alternative is what neuroscientist Professor Darcia Narvaez calls sleep nudging.

What is sleep nudging?

Sleep nudging is not about shutting down your baby by ignoring their communication. It's about nudging your child to sleep within their tolerance and not outside of it. It is important that your child feels secure throughout the process. Firstly, says Professor Navaez, do not attempt sleep nudging before your child is six months old. In their first year of life, the social and emotional processing parts of your baby's brain – in other words, the foundation for their mental health – are wiring up in relationship with your loving interaction. So do not start this process before they are ready. And all babies are different as to when they may be ready.

As I mentioned earlier, babies aren't born with the capacity to believe that an object still exists when they can't see it; psychotherapists call this 'object permanence'. So when they are left alone, they may feel abandoned. Our own sense of people continuing to exist even when we cannot see or hear them is so ingrained it's easy to overlook that we had to learn it too.

Once a baby does have this sense of 'object permanence' – and, again, I'm not going to say when this is, as we all develop at different speeds and it is possible to have the knowledge of permanence cognitively but not feel it on a bodily level until later – it's easier to begin to nudge for more separation at night.

The first step is to notice where and when your baby feels safe and secure as they fall asleep. This may be going to sleep while breastfeeding and being nursed back to sleep if they wake up. This 'comfort baseline', as Narvaez calls it, is where you need to start.

Next, what is the smallest step you can take to move away from the baseline? It may be to stop nursing while they are still drowsy but not yet asleep and cuddle them instead so they can still feel your body and your heartbeat. If your baby accepts this step, repeat it so it becomes the new comfort baseline before going on to the next step or nudge: a further separating step such as lying them down when they become drowsy and stroking their forehead, or whatever soothes your baby. The next step might be to move the baby out of the bed and into a cot right next to it. Then going on to move the cot further away, and eventually into another room. At any stage, if your baby becomes distressed, you return to their comfort baseline.

My story:

> My first nudge was to stop nursing when my daughter was still drowsy and cuddle her. When that became her baseline, the next nudge was to pass her over to her father to cuddle her to sleep. With that arrangement, we could have one adult sleeping with her while the other got some sleep in another room.
>
> When she was about two, she asked for her own room but was aghast when it came to night-time and we suggested she should sleep in it alone. 'Oh, not to sleep in, only to play in,' she said. We gave her another nudge by saying we would stay with her until she was asleep and, if she woke up, she could come into our bed, so long as she didn't wake us up and there was no talking. She accepted this arrangement and sometimes we woke up with our daughter in the bed with us and sometimes we didn't.
>
> By the time she was three she only ever slept in her own room, and when she was four she was happy and secure enough to start to put herself to bed, which she did of her own volition, with no nudging. Although this was on her terms: she got to choose whether she put herself to bed or asked one of us to be with her as she got ready. She didn't resist going to bed because it had always been a place of comfort, not of loneliness.

The important thing is, you make each of these nudges within your child's baseline of comfort. We all develop at different speeds and have different needs for closeness and for our own space, so when the time is right will depend on your baby. What felt fine with your first child might not be the case with the next. What you want is for your child to associate their bed with relief from tiredness, with comfort, cosiness and sleep rather than separation, loneliness and desperation. If bed is about good things, they will not be reluctant to go there. This will help them get enough sleep throughout their childhood, which, as you know, is important for their development.

Doing the sleep-nudge process (rather than sleep training), using encouragement rather than punishment will take longer, but I believe it's worth it. The result will be more long-lasting and makes separating to go to bed easier for children as they develop, and it contributes to a good relationship between you and your child. Being encouraged to do anything is fine for a relationship, but being tricked, ignored or manipulated into a behaviour is not going to enhance your lifelong bond. I do understand how difficult it is to take the long-term view when you are exhausted but, again, I believe it is worth it.

Many of the things we expect our children to achieve, they will, with the minimum guidance or from following our example. Nudging them to the edge of their comfort zone but not beyond it is often a way forward if they do need some help. Remember that, if we do something that they can do for themselves, we may be disempowering them.

Helping, not rescuing

When the child is in charge of how they separate, they are less likely to become insecure and clingy than when the parents leave them before they are ready. This goes for separation at night, being left alone at nursery, going to a party on their own and any other situation where they are without you. You can 'nudge' to encourage a child to accept these situations – that is, go to the edge of their comfort baseline – but if you are in too much of a hurry for a child to become independent, it will end up in extra work because it can damage your relationship and you will need to repair it. You may see making them manage without you as encouraging independence, but they are more likely to feel it as being pushed away and experience it as some sort of punishment. My message here is to trust your child to separate at their pace and to follow their pace, rather than imposing yours.

In their own good time, your child will sleep all night and on their own, they will sit up, crawl, walk, get themselves dressed, eat solids, cook their own breakfast and pay their own rent. When we push them to do things before they are ready, we frustrate them and ourselves. Many things we painstakingly teach them or make them do they would have picked up on their own in their own time anyway. In our rush to move their development along we may even delay it.

For example, when we prop up a baby into a sitting position rather than wait for them to push themselves up, we deny them the opportunity to learn to do this for themselves. A baby does not need props that restrict their movement in order to sit; all they need is time and space to discover movement. Left to their own devices, they will roll and wriggle, learn how to crawl, to sit up, to stand and to walk for themselves. They will also be learning how to learn. We do not have to interfere with these processes.

In fact, a baby who is often propped up before they can naturally sit up, before the right muscles have developed, sometimes won't learn to crawl properly but instead will learn a sort of lopsided shuffle from a sitting position which can interfere with naturally good posture later. I'm afraid this was the fate of my own daughter. Never mind: you cannot get everything right. I am conscious that when I talk about 'best practice' parenting, you may have already been through the stage I describe and you'll feel bad because you did something different. But what matters is your relationship, not how soon you started to wean or that you propped your baby up too early. My daughter goes to Pilates now she is an adult and is correcting her posture. It would have been great if I'd had the information when I needed it, but

I didn't. I will keep saying this: it isn't the mistake that matters as much as making amends for it, even if the amends is Pilates or any other type of therapy your child needs when they are older. Please don't feel shame if your child needs any sort of help when they are adults because of something you got wrong when they were younger. Being defensive about our mistakes will make them worse, not make them disappear.

The sitting example may sound quite specific, but it's to make a general point about how much to help: don't disempower your child by doing something they could learn to do themselves, especially if you back off a bit. You may find the concept of nudging or encouragement helpful when deciding how much to help.

> Freya, aged five months, two weeks and three days old, is lying on her front on a rug in the sitting room. Her father is on the sofa close by, reading. Freya makes a squawk; she is trying to grab a ping-pong ball that is on the floor just out of reach. Dad looks up and sees her problem. Should he fix it? She looks up at him and lets out a frustrated cry. 'You really want that ball, don't you?' says Dad, as he kneels on the floor next to her. 'Can you reach it?' He smiles at her encouragingly, he looks at her, then he looks at the ball. Freya stops crying and begins to bring her knees up and manages to wriggle towards the ball by pulling herself up on her hands. She lies down again and stretches towards the ball. Her fingers touch it and it goes further away. Dad puts it back where it was and Freya tries again; this time she grabs it and squeals with delight and Dad laughs along with her. 'You tried really hard then. Well done,' he says.

Of course, it's difficult to know, as a parent in a scenario like this, whether to rescue, to encourage or just to observe. By watching your baby or your child for cues, you will be able to get it right a lot of the time. If you rescue them when they could do something for themselves, you are disempowering them and robbing them of agency, but if you don't help them when they are helpless, you are not being sensitive towards them. In the above example, Freya's dad gets it just right. He does this naturally, without thinking about it, because it was done that way for him. If it was not done like this for you, it's a good idea to consciously adopt this style.

> **Exercise: Let your child take the lead**
>
> Get into the habit of being with your child, not doing anything but keeping them company and following their lead. Think about observing and helping them rather than just rescuing. Help them problem-solve rather than doing it for them.

Play

The very word implies that play is trivial – but it is vitally important. While playing, an infant learns to concentrate and gets in the habit of making discoveries, one of which is the joy of feeling absorbed by what they are doing. In addition, they learn how to connect ideas and feed their imagination. It's also through play that children learn how to connect with their peers. Play is the foundation for creativity and for work; for exploration and discovery. All mammals play, because play is practice for life. Playing is your baby's and your child's work – and needs to be respected as such.

I was surprised when I first read the work of Maria Montessori that she said a child who is concentrating on an activity must not be interrupted. I wasn't used to the idea that when a toddler is pushing a truck around the carpet and making a noise like an engine they are in fact working. They are absorbed, they are concentrating, they are using their imagination, they are constructing a narrative; their activity has a beginning, a middle and an end. And when allowed to repeat such processes many times, they lay down a solid foundation for completing tasks and concentrating.

A child's work starts earlier than this stage, though. Your baby needs a safe place to play so they can touch all the objects within their reach. If they are being told 'no' all the time, their concentration will be broken. An undistracted baby can play for minutes at a time with a simple object like a piece of tissue paper. They can learn how to grab it, screw it up, drop it, reach for it again. A baby does not get bored with an activity, even if you do. While this is going on, your job is just to watch, to follow their gaze but not to direct it.

Children don't need a lot of toys. As you probably know, the cliché of them preferring the box to the article inside it is so often true. A two-year-old child of my acquaintance was given a great pile of toys by her doting parents, friends and relations on her birthday. One of her aunts also threw in an empty plastic lemon-juice bottle shaped like a lemon. What was the child's favourite toy? The lemon bottle, of course! Playing with this, she learned how to suck water into it and push water out of it and to direct the jet of water too. So, the fancy dolls' house went largely unplayed with, and so did the Disney characters and the tiny kitchen and whatever other landfill had been bought for her. Children do not need more than a few simple toys: a couple of toy cars, a cardboard box, a square of material, a doll, a bear and a few bricks, and a child is set up. Some dressing-up clothes can fire imagination too. More is not better. If they only have a few toys – one drawer or chest of toys, and some craft materials such as paint and paper – then each thing can have its place to be returned to after play.

Children, just like adults, become overwhelmed and frozen when given too much choice. We might believe we'd prefer to have lots of options, but experiments by the psychologist Barry Schwartz show that we don't. In one, he found people felt happier with a box containing a choice of six chocolates rather than a choice of thirty – and were more satisfied with the chocolate they chose. What happens when we have too much choice is we worry we'll make the wrong one. The average child in the West has more than 150 toys and receives an extra 70 to add to this number every year. This is overwhelming for children. With too many toys, they're more likely to flit from activity to activity rather than engage deeply in one. Buying more toys is often indulged in by parents because they hope it will mean that the child will want them less. But guess what? It doesn't work.

Children need free play where they choose and direct their own activity to build their capacity for creativity. But sometimes a child wants you to play with them. And it is you they need, not the novelty of a new toy.

You might feel it's time-consuming and it may not be your idea of fun to play 'show party' or whatever game they devise for you to join in. It can be frustrating when a child demands that you play, especially if you have a pile of stuff to get on with. However, I found investing my energy at the beginning of play-time paid off. When my daughter wanted me involved, she'd demand that I 'Talk teddy'. Then she'd gradually take over and do the talking for teddy herself.

Play is a time to let the child take the lead, to decide on an activity and direct your role in that activity. You're more likely to be able to tackle that pile of stuff if you help your child to start their play and gradually back off as they become more self-absorbed. It is easier for you and nicer for them if you play with them first.

On the other hand, if you tell your child you're too busy to play with them, they are likely to continually interrupt you so you don't have time to do your work. You're also giving them the message that they're boring or a nuisance, and this might make them feel lonely, angry or sad, even insecure about their relationship with you. Once a child has started playing and is content, they can continue their play without having to check on you or keep you engaged.

You have to put the time in anyway with children. Invest it

positively at the beginning, then you're less likely to have to invest it negatively later. This is true of playtime as well as many other times.

The other day I was watching a father and daughter on the beach. The girl looked to be around the age of six. When they first arrived, it was 'Daddy, do this,' 'Come with me,' 'Come to the water,' 'Get the bucket,' 'Build this.' Daddy did everything he was told. After a while, the girl became more and more absorbed and involved in playing with the wet sand where the tide had gone out. Daddy was close by but only observing, not participating – and he managed to read his newspaper as well. It was a lovely example of the girl gradually finding her inner 'autopilot' so Daddy could get a bit of leisure too.

After a while another girl came and stood and watched her for a bit, and she started to involve that child in her game. It was satisfying to watch. If Daddy had not started off playing with her and had gone to his newspaper straightaway, she may have been preoccupied with her relationship with him, may have become fretful and couldn't have allowed herself to become so absorbed or make a new friend.

Most children also like some organized games like cricket or cards as part of family time together. You may associate such games with love and enjoy passing them on. But if you weren't played with as a child, you may find that playing or even organizing these games feels like too much. Be aware if playing is bringing up some feelings from the past in you. You can either overcome these feelings by knowing they don't belong in the present or make sure that other children or adults are around to help facilitate play and try to join in occasionally.

I remember, once, we were one of three families spending time together in the days between Christmas and New Year. The Monopoly board was brought out, much to the amusement of most of the adults and the enthusiasm of the children. But one of the dads got up and went to get his coat, declaring he was going to walk the four miles home and leave the car for his wife and son. I followed him into the hall. He told me he was an only child. He was always given board games for Christmas but no one ever bothered to play with him. So these games always brought up such sadness in him that he said, if he stayed, he was frightened he would spoil it for everyone. I haven't really got a happy ending for this story, I'm afraid, but what struck me at the time was how much what is laid down in childhood can stick.

Children thrive when they have multi-aged playmates. Put a couple of very young toddlers together and they'll be more likely to have parallel play than to play with each other. Age-mixed play teaches children how to play in a way that playing with kids of their own age does not. Younger children can learn more from older friends than they would by just mixing with their peers. Most of our learning comes from observing others; older children teach younger ones more sophisticated behaviour and are role models, and they can offer more emotional support to younger children too. And the older children learn how to teach, how to nurture and how to be leaders.

Looking back over their childhood, many adults feel their happiest times were when there were children of all ages who they could make up games with, run around with and had plenty of space to do it in. These times usually happened on holiday, with cousins, friends, on camping trips, at festivals, on days out or days near home at a park or in a garden. And they included having trusted adults there in the background to go to if necessary, providing meals and enough boundaries to make them feel safe. I worry that with too many structured after-school activities children may not be getting enough time in a mixed-aged group to organize their own play. Most children probably need more time outside with other children and less time inside being organized or in front of screens. Screens should be used with caution. They can become addictive, but denying them altogether is another sort of deprivation.

Exercise: Creating great play habits

- Don't interrupt a concentrating child.
- When a younger child wants to play with you, start them off on the activity they choose. Then, when they get so absorbed they don't need you, back off.
- With older children, don't feel you must be the entertainments officer every time your child doesn't know what to do. When a child is bored, have faith and tell them you have confidence in them that they will find something fun to do. Boredom may be a necessary component of creativity.
- Do, however, put some time aside for enjoying yourself with your children by sharing activities you enjoy – board games, card games, sports, singing or whatever you like.
- Children thrive with playmates of all ages.

PART SIX

Behaviour: All Behaviour is Communication

I've put the section on behaviour last because it's so much easier to behave better when the other things I've been talking about are taken care of. That includes, for a child, having their feelings considered as part of their supportive, loving relationships. We all behave better when we're not desperate for more contact and connection, when we feel we belong.

The hand that rocks the cradle *does* rule the world. We owe it to the world to love more than we judge and to consider our children's feelings rather than automatically dismissing them as silly or wrong. Treating infants and children with consideration and respect doesn't mean you don't set boundaries.

In this part, we will look at the winning and losing game, the qualities we need to develop to behave well, how strict a parent should be, clinging and whingeing and when to set boundaries and how to set them.

Role models

Your child will ape your behaviour, if not now, eventually. I once had a client who explained to me how very different he was from his father, who ran large corporations for profit in the top-down manner of an autocrat. But although my client worked in the charity sector, his way of running his department was – you've guessed it – autocratic. Our own behaviour is probably the biggest influence on our child's behaviour. We think we are individuals, but we all affect each other. We are but parts of a system, and the roles we carve out for ourselves will be in reaction to the parts other people play around us. So, however your child behaves or how you behave, it is not in isolation, it is co-created by the people and culture around you too.

How would you describe your behaviour? Are you respectful to other human beings all the time? Do you consider their feelings? Does your 'good behaviour' go deep or is it merely manners? Are you pleasant on the surface, but do you then condemn people behind their backs? Do you get stuck in relentless games of one-upmanship? However you behave, you'll be teaching your children to behave like that too, including any behaviour you don't approve of.

If you consistently behave with kind consideration towards your children and towards other people, then your children will probably follow suit . . . eventually. In the meantime, your children might not behave 'well' all the time, because before language, behaviour is the only way they can communicate what is going on for them. And this remains true even for quite a few years after they develop language too. That's because it takes some practice and skill to know what it is we're feeling, to put it into words and then to work out from that what we need. Even adults – nay, even poets – can find this hard.

I don't believe there is anyone who is all good or all bad. I'll go even further: I would say that the concepts of 'good' and 'bad' are not useful. It is true, although quite rare, that some people are born without the capacity to feel empathy, no matter how much is shown to them. But having a differently wired brain does not mean you are in any way 'bad'. I will only relent on this good-and-evil argument so far as to say that some people's behaviour is inconvenient or harmful to others. No one is born bad. So rather than label behaviour as 'good' or 'bad', I describe it as 'convenient' or 'inconvenient'.

Behaviour, as I've said, is purely communication. People – and especially children – act out in inappropriate, inconvenient ways because they haven't found alternative, more effective, more convenient ways of expressing their feelings and needs. Some children's behaviour is inconvenient to others, but it is not 'bad'.

Your job is to decipher your child's behaviour. Rather than dividing our children up into 'good' bits and 'bad' bits, there are questions you need to ask. What is their behaviour trying to say? Can you help them to communicate in a more convenient way? What are they telling you with their bodies, with their noises and with whatever words they may choose? And, a really hard question to ask yourself: how is their behaviour co-created with yours?

The winning and losing game

Once, when my daughter, Flo, was three years old she wanted to walk the short way to the shops and not go in her pushchair so I left the pushchair at home. On the way back she just stopped and sat down on someone's front step. My instinct was to think, 'Oh no!' because, in my mind, I was more in the future than in the present; I was already putting away the shopping so I could relax and rest. It wasn't in my plan to rest halfway home. But Flo was resting now.

Then I realized that it didn't matter when we got home. I put down the bags and crouched beside her. Flo was looking at an ant following a crack in the pavement. Sometimes it disappeared into the crack and then it got out again. I watched with her.

An elderly man came up to us and said to me, 'Is she winning?' I knew what he meant straightaway. He meant, in the battle of the wills between parent and child, was she getting her way at my expense? I knew this battle of old. My parents believed in it to the extent that they thought if any child got too much of what they wanted, whatever it was, it would be bad for them.

But you and your child are on the same side: you both want to feel content rather than frustrated. You both want to get along and behave well. The old man smiled knowingly down on us. He was only trying to be friendly, so I didn't argue. I didn't say something like, 'We are in a relationship, not in a battle.' I just said, 'We are watching an ant,' and smiled back at him. He went on his way, and so did the ant. Flo and I stood up and went on our way too.

As I said above, all behaviour is communication, so behind behaviour you'll find the feelings. Once you discover the feeling behind any particular behaviour and empathize with it, then you can put the feeling into words, you will help a child use words to express themselves and they will have less need to act out on that feeling.

In the example above I realized that Flo, unused to walking for so long, was tired and wanted to rest. I thought about how she might have been overwhelmed by all the sights and sounds around her – she might not have learned how to block out the ones not relevant to her, as an adult automatically does, and that may have been behind her need to focus on just one thing. It is more useful to think of a situation from the child's point of view rather than yours. Mine here would have been: I want to get home; she is stopping me; it is my will against hers.

Traditionally, it was thought that you must not let children 'get their own way'. I think this is what the old man was trying to say with his 'Is she winning?' remark. He was going down the 'You are making a rod for your own back' approach. I hear about this all the time when people talk about tantrums. Parents seem to fear tantrums so much that even to notice one, they think, will mean that a child will never grow out of having them. In this don't-let-them-win game that parents play, there are no winners. There is only manipulation rather than relating to each other. The game is not real. It is something parents make up.

Such an approach is based on a fantasy of what will happen in the future rather than what is working in the present. What was working in that present was Flo resting before continuing with our walk.

The game of winning and losing can get entrenched as a dynamic and this damages relationships. By dominating a child, you teach them to dominate. What if your child gets into the pattern of thinking it's normal and desirable to impose their will on to other people? How popular will that make them with their classmates?

If you act as though a large part of childcare is imposing your will over your children, the patterns of relating that your child will learn from that have the potential to be harmful. If a child learns such a limited choice of roles – 'the doer' and the 'done to', or to put it another way, the dominant and the submissive – it considerably limits their potential as a person. For example, if the roles they have had the most experience of are victim and bully, they may either become a bully or start to automatically find themselves in the victim role.

The game of winning and losing also has consequences for the emotional repertoire of your child. To lose a battle of wills can often mean humiliation. And the consequence of being humiliated is not, as the word might imply, that a person becomes humble but that they become angry. That anger may be turned inwards towards the self, leading to depression, or outwards towards the world, which results in antisocial behaviour.

So, if it's not about winning and losing, what is the best way to think about helping a child behave appropriately and conveniently at any one time? Generally, going with what works in the present, which is grounded in reality rather than what you fear may happen in the future, based on fantasy, is a useful maxim to live by with children.

Going with what is working in the present rather than what you fantasize may happen in the future

A client of mine, Gina, was weaning her daughter. The only way she could get her to eat was by singing to her while the child ate her vegetables and spaghetti sitting on her special rug in the middle of the room. Doing this, the kid was happy and, because the food was going in, my client was happy too.

Sometimes we tell ourselves stories about the future: what if the only way she can ever eat is when she is sung to at the same time? What if he never learns to sleep in his own bed? What if she never wants to give up her pacifier? What if Mr Squidgy has to accompany him to the office on his first day at work? But these stories are just that: stories. In the example above, if Gina had thought, 'What if this is the only way my daughter will ever eat? What if she'll always refuse to eat at a table?' she could have worried about, say, school lunchtimes, restaurants, even her daughter's first date. But, believe me, almost everything with children is a phase. So it's fine to go with what works in the present, however odd it seems.

I think going with what works for everyone right now is especially useful when it comes to sleep. If the only way everyone gets some sleep is if you push two double beds together and pile the whole family in, then don't worry about tomorrow: get some sleep tonight. Eventually, your children will want their own beds. They'll get fed up with your snoring.

If what is working stops working, then implement a change, but make it one where everyone wins, as far as possible, or at least one where there are no winners or losers. Modelling flexibility will make this easier.

The qualities we need to behave well

As I said above, your job is to model good behaviour, to behave towards your child and towards other people with the same empathetic attitude and hope your child will adopt this behaviour too. As well as that, there are four skills we all need to develop in order to become socialized, to behave conveniently. These are:

1. Being able to tolerate frustration
2. Flexibility
3. Problem-solving skills
4. The ability to see and feel things from other people's point of view

To put these into context, I managed to (1) tolerate my frustration when Flo wanted to sit down on a step on the way back from the shops when I wanted to get home. I was (2) flexible because I changed my expectation about the speed of the progress we would make on our walk back. I solved the problem (3) of Flo needing a rest by allowing her to have one and (4) I used my ability to see how wanting to stop might feel from Flo's perspective. And, indeed, I managed to see the situation from the old man's point of view as well, thus I managed to behave conveniently for both Flo and the old man.

Some children naturally pick up the four skills of socialized behaviour because they automatically mimic those around them. But children vary enormously at what age they reach any milestones, including these. Some children can read before they are three; I couldn't read with any fluency until I was nine. Some can run about before they are one and others still prefer to crawl at eighteen months. And just as physical skills are learned at differing ages, children develop each of their behavioural skills at different times to their peers too.

I often hear parents say that their child is 'driving them mad!', which translates as 'I cannot stop my child from screaming/ crying/whining/demanding' or whatever behaviour is pushing their buttons. I believe when children behave in a way you find inconvenient, it cannot be considered a choice in the way an adult makes a choice. Children want to be loved by you, they want to connect, they want to be friends. Sometimes they want your attention so much that getting negative attention from you is better than getting no attention.

It helps, when it comes to managing your own emotions around your child, if you can understand the emotion and the circumstances that caused your child to behave in the way you're finding hard to deal with.

Some children appear to be difficult to understand and to soothe from the beginning. It could be colic or some other dis-comfort such as not liking lights or noise, or having a full nappy, or being scared or tired, or being very sensitive, or lots of other things. Often we may have no idea of the cause of their distress, but that doesn't mean we shouldn't try to soothe them. Alterna-tively, your child might have been easy to soothe as a baby but may have difficulties dealing with self-control later on. Soothing them and accepting them at whatever stage they are at is more likely to help to nudge them along to the next stage than losing patience with them.

Often, frustration in a child comes when the challenge to do something is too great and the child can't handle it. A child is most frustrated just before they master a new stage or skill. Before they can walk, talk, think, write, be sexual, be independ-ent, they're at their most brittle. You can think of the child's inconvenient outburst or tantrum or sulk as a developmental milestone that has not yet been reached rather than a planned, intentional intervention on their part. If you watch a child have a tantrum, they are not enjoying it. No one would choose to feel like that if they felt they had a choice about it.

Another thing that's often said is that children behave in a way that's inconvenient to others because their parents are lax. This isn't true: many lax parents manage to have children whose behaviour is not a problem to themselves or to others, and stricter parents may have children who, despite the consistency and fairness of their mothers and fathers, behave inconveniently. Sometimes, whether a kid behaves conveniently or not is not so much to do with whether their parents are strict or lax, it's more about the speed they pick up those four skills: tolerance of frustration, flexibility, problem-solving skills and ability to consider others.

How to learn to behave conveniently rather than in an antisocial manner is not an exact science. What causes one child to behave appropriately might not bring forth the same results in another. Children are people, not machines. We want them to be able to connect and relate rather than become robots. I am not a fan of sticker charts or bribes because they are more about judging behaviour than relating. From them, children learn neither tolerance for frustration, nor flexibility, nor problem-solving skills, nor how to think and feel for other people. Behaviour charts are manipulative. They are a trick. If we manipulate children, we cannot complain if they learn how to manipulate us and others. I believe in relating to children rather than conditioning them to want star stickers.

When we behave well, it's rarely because we want a reward or because we fear punishment, it's because behaving with consideration towards other people comes naturally to us. It's because we have learned that collaboration leads to a more harmonious life than opposition does. We don't do favours for other people or consider their feelings because we fear punishment if we don't; we help people because we want to make life easier for them. We want our children to act with consideration and empathy towards others rather than being motivated only by the narrower ideas of punishment and material reward. Having said that, I do not know a single parent, including myself, who has not resorted to a bribe at one point or another, but bribes should be the exception, not the norm.

The best way of getting your kids interested in chores, for example filling and emptying the dishwasher, is to let them play with whatever it is when they are toddlers (remember: play is work). They will keep imitating you when you cooperate with their play and they will cooperate with you and, after what can seem, I admit, a long time, you have a person in your house who empties the dishwasher because they want to contribute, not because you are bribing them to empty it. Some people believe in paying their children to do chores to teach them, they say, the value of money. However, I believe to teach a child the value of money we need to teach them the value of people.

Children learn their behaviour from how they are treated. They really learn how to say 'please' and 'thank you' when gratitude and respect have been shown to them. They can then embody it. If you only drill your child into saying these things, they may never learn to feel them. We can feel embarrassed as parents when someone gives our child a present and they don't say 'thank you' because we want everyone to love our children as much as we do and we do not want them to reflect badly on us, but we need to put our narcissism to one side and, rather than humiliate our child by getting them to say something they might not feel, we can give thanks for the present ourselves so the giver doesn't feel unappreciated. Children learn real gratitude when they are shown it. It starts by you welcoming those pretend cups of tea they want to hand you for hours at a time. They are not wasted hours. They are invested hours.

If all behaviour is communication, what does this or that inconvenient behaviour mean?

So how can you understand what your child's current inconvenient behaviour might mean? Start with thinking about when you're at your worst. I know I'm at my worst when people around me don't understand me and do not even seem to be trying to understand me; I find it a strain to behave well if I need someone's attention and they are ignoring me; I feel stressed when an expectation, a hope or a plan I have is dashed due to things outside my control, when I'm expected to achieve something I find impossible, or when I'm in a situation I can no longer tolerate. When your child acts out in frustration, it is probably due to similar circumstances. They may cry or sulk or scream, kick, hit, throw things or even throw themselves about so much they hurt themselves.

Make a note as to when they act out in this way. What are their triggers? What frustrations do they have the most difficulty with? Is your mood another factor in the mix? You need to be the one who observes because, if you ask them, they may not know why they reacted like they did. They'll probably say something like 'It's not fair' or even 'I don't know.'

The problem is, when we are upset, that feeling of being upset is so predominant it's difficult to articulate it. And when very young it's even more difficult for a child to articulate why they find some situations difficult or impossible to cope with. Sometimes, this can apply to us as parents as well as our children. Let's have a look at the following example. It's an email I received from Gina, who has a nursery-aged daughter called Aoife.

> Tonight, I got stuck on a train for an hour coming from London so I didn't get to nursery to pick up Aoife until 5.40, over half an hour late. When I got there she was fine, playing nicely with a

little boy. But as soon as we left she began to be . . . I am just going to say it because this is what I'm thinking . . . so naughty. She ran up and down the corridor screaming, 'No, no, no!' when I asked her to put on her coat. I felt completely out of control, like she was running rings around me. I was so embarrassed in front of the other parents. For the sake of trying to sound effective, I told her she wouldn't get a pudding that night if she carried on . . . but of course it made no difference.

Nobody else's child at nursery acts like this. Aoife always looks like the naughty one. Outside, she was just as bad. She wouldn't get in the buggy, she wouldn't put on her hat, or her gloves. I had to go to the chemist's, where she wouldn't hold my hand then kept pulling things off the shelves. At the counter she started screaming and shouting. Trying to get her in the buggy, we ended up almost wrestling while she was screaming. Again, I felt out of control and completely useless because my child was being naughty and I couldn't control her.

When I got to the corner of our road I realized, having tried to put Aoife's coat on her for so long, I'd left my shopping bag with the supper in it in the nursery porch. I ran back but it was all locked up. I felt despairing. I was so angry with Aoife, the angriest I have ever been with her because I was going to look even more stupid and like a crap parent at nursery.

When we got home and I saw my partner I burst into tears. I was literally standing with my back to Aoife, sobbing. That also made me feel terrible because who cries in front of their child? Why am I such a bad parent?

This is what I wrote back:

How awful to be delayed by a stuck train for a whole hour. If it was me, I would have been so stressed and frustrated and miserable, imagining how horrible it was that I was going to be late for pick-up. I'd be so worried that the nursery would think I was uncaring because I was so late. I'd be worried that my daughter might be worried too. Knowing how I can work myself up about stuff like that, I'd be on edge and would need for everything else to go smoothly, for routine to be re-established. So, I'd be in such a rush to get back on track that I wouldn't have anything left to think about how Aoife would be feeling. I'd try to make her behave too because I wouldn't have one jot of emotional energy left to slow down to try and find out what Aoife's feelings were and to work out how to soothe her. I would feel mortified if other people, instead of witnessing love and co-operation between us, saw my child having a tantrum and me apparently not being able to do anything about it. (I can also say, now I have some distance from the toddler years, that we have all been there.) I'd feel terrible that I'd issued a threat. Then forgetting the shopping – it would have been too much for me to hold it all together. I too would have burst into tears as soon as I'd found the safe arms of someone who knows and loves me.

Now, I'm going to imagine what it's like for Aoife:

Hi, Mum. I can't write yet and even my talking is on the limited side, but if I could explain myself, this is what I'd say:

It would really help if, instead of judging me as being 'naughty' and explaining me away that way, you tried instead to work out what is going on between us.

At nursery, I had an underlying feeling of uneasiness because it felt like you should have been there already and I should have been with you. Then, when you did come, I was playing a complicated game. You told me we were leaving right this minute and to put on my coat. I said, 'No.' Then you insisted and then I screamed and then you weren't happy. It did not go well.

Let's look at why I said 'No.' I have got into the habit of saying it when things go too fast for me and I want them to slow down. I'm not trying to be difficult or manipulative, it's just an automatic reaction because I hate sudden changes that I'm not expecting. You were so distracted and rushed that I couldn't get a connection with you and that scared me, and when I get scared I get angry too. You are always thinking about what needs to happen in the future, but I live in the present and I need you to be in the present with me, otherwise I feel alone and get upset.

When you were late, I needed you to slow down and explain what had happened to make you late. Then I needed you to explain what was going to happen next so I could get my head round it. I haven't yet learned how to be flexible so I need more time than you do when it comes to shifting gears. Putting on my coat AND stopping what I was in the middle of was just too much for me at once. I bet if you were in the middle of a complicated piece of work, which is what playing is for me, you would be frustrated if you were interrupted.

What I need when you want me to stop doing something, whatever it is, whether it's playing or running about, is a warning. I need a specific warning for each thing: to stop playing, to put on my coat, to get in the pushchair. I need a space to take each thing in too. Tell me what the plan is when you know it and give me a chance to take it in and understand. I might need a five-minute warning before I need to stop playing, and to be told I might find it hard. Then a three-minute warning. Then a one-minute warning. If I still cannot bear the thought of putting on my coat when we are inside, carry my coat outside and ask me to put it on there. One gear change I really hate is when I have to go from running about to getting in the pushchair. There is nowhere for my energy to go so it just bursts out of me in frustration.

When you tell me not to say 'No' or to stop running around or shouting and tell me what the consequence will be, it doesn't help. That's because I haven't yet picked up the skill of looking ahead to the possible outcomes of how I behave. Those neural pathways will fire up in due course. At the moment, when you're telling me off it makes me think you don't understand, then I get more scared and more angry and have to say 'No' all the more. When I feel overwhelmed, I can't be still and quiet.

What would help is if you could try to identify my difficulty and say it in a way that makes sense for me. For example, 'You are feeling frustrated because you don't want to stop this fun game.' By you putting my frustrations and fears into words, I will start to learn to use words too. Then I will be able to communicate better and be less likely to lose control.

If you get cross, or tell me I'm being silly, I will just close down or scream. I know it's hard for you when you're stressed and in a hurry to think about relating with me rather than just getting me to do stuff or to behave in a certain way. But when we have a to-and-fro exchange where I feel met and seen and loved and understood, then I feel calm and my feelings don't burst from me in the form of inconvenient behaviour.

At the chemist's, if you had told me what you were thinking and doing, I could have helped you. But because you just told me to be good, I copied you and got things from the shelves. Please include me in tasks, even though you think you have not got time. It takes a long time anyway because at the moment you spend that time admonishing me.

Even though you were crying, Daddy loved you and gave you a cuddle. How nice it was that he understood about forgetting the shopping. That's what I need too. If we'd had a cuddle at nursery when I was upset because I had to stop playing I think we both could have managed better. Mum, because you know you and me are together for ever, superficially you care more about what other people might be thinking. I understand this, but it isn't helpful when you judge yourself through their eyes.

One day soon, Mum, I will be able to tolerate frustration, be flexible about plans, I will be able to put my feelings into words rather than behave inconveniently and I will also learn to take your feelings on board too, because I'll learn that from you thinking about mine.

And don't worry about being good or bad at parenting. You are the best mummy in the world and the only one I ever, ever want.

Investing time positively earlier rather than negatively later

Being a parent is always going to be time consuming. It is better to put in that time positively by pre-empting trouble rather than negatively, after the trouble has arisen. If you go too fast for the pace of your child, if you don't verbalize their feelings for them, if you don't give them warnings about your plans, if you don't include them in any tasks, you will instead find you spend the time you thought you had saved telling them off instead. There's no getting around having to invest time in your child, so why not invest it positively? I'm happy to report that as Gina learned to slow down, to stay in contact with Aoife by staying in the present and began to see situations from her point of view and put them simply into words for her, Aoife's behaviour became more convenient.

Exercise: how to predict difficulties

If you want to change a situation your child often finds difficult, or you know there's a potentially tricky new situation coming up, it can really help to stop and imagine what it is like to be your child and to imagine what they would say if they could identify their feelings, articulate them – and knew what would help. Try writing it down in the form of a letter to yourself from your child or baby's point of view, like I did above. Writing it down can really help you get into your child's mindset – and that can make it clearer how both of you can have a calmer time.

Helping behaviour by putting feelings into words

It's helpful when we want a child (or anyone!) to stop one behaviour if we suggest an alternative way of being, as happens in the following example:

John's four-year-old, Junior, used to wake up every single morning, start screaming, run to his parents' bedroom and carry on screaming at them until he was given a cuddle.

One morning, John suggested to his son he might like to try a new tactic, of coming into their bedroom without screaming. He told Junior, 'You can just say, "Good morning, Mum and Dad, I would like a cuddle, please." ' Junior tried to do this, but there were still tears.

Junior's mum asked him, 'Do you feel lonely when you wake up?' and he nodded. They suggested he could say this instead: 'Good morning, Mum and Dad. I'm lonely and I'd like a cuddle, please.' This turned things around. Junior began to bounce into the bedroom every morning, say his new sentence and get a cuddle.

After a few days, the parents said, 'You don't seem lonely. You can be happy and still get a cuddle too!' In the end, Junior had a new morning sentence: 'I'm okay, and I want a cuddle.'

John and Junior's story illustrates how putting feelings into words can really shift them along. This is true for adults, too.

It can feel hard, as a parent, to acknowledge your child's feeling beneath tears and screams because you don't want to think that your child is suffering. To name the suffering feels like it will make it worse, but it doesn't, it usually makes it better. It takes time to put things into words but when a child is upset they'll find it even harder to find the words, so it is up to you.

When Flo was a toddler I used to take her swimming at the local pool. One day I couldn't go, so my husband took her instead.

Their swimming session went well until it was time to leave and my husband turned to go up the stairs. The way we usually went into the pool was via the stairs and the way we usually left the pool was via the lift. So Flo, then aged twenty-two months, said, 'No,' and sat on the floor.

This was inconvenient behaviour. It fits the normal definition of 'bad' behaviour, but Flo wasn't behaving badly, she just wanted the routine to be as it always was. She hadn't yet learned flexibility, or how to articulate clearly what she wanted. Instead of taking the time to find out what the 'no' was about, my hurried, harassed husband picked her up to take her up the stairs, which is not what she wanted at all, so she started to scream. By the time they got home they were both very cross. After I heard this tale I looked into her big blue eyes, still brimming with tears, and said, 'You were looking forward to pressing the lift button, weren't you?' A little nod. 'And Dad didn't know that's why you wanted to go in the lift and not use the stairs, did he?' A shake of the head.

What we learned from this experience is that if you are going to deviate from a normal, much-loved routine, it's probably necessary to give lots of warning, some imagining and possibly even some rehearsing.

When explanations are unhelpful

I was lucky in that I was able to guess what went wrong. But often situations arise and you can't guess. Maybe you've taken your child to something you wanted to be lovely, like going swimming, but it has all ended in tears and it seems impossible to work out why.

It's natural for you to look for some sort of certainty about why a child is crying or shouting or refusing to do something – otherwise, you feel out of control – but it is really okay not to know and to stay curious. The reason parents fall back on most is 'Oh, it's because they're tired,' which may or may not be a factor in the mix. But I can remember, as a child, hearing this explanation, and it added to my fury because it wasn't an accurate mirror of what I was feeling so it left me feeling misunderstood. The 'tired' explanation is much loved by parents, but I think we know who is truly tired, and I don't mean the kid!

There are some other interpretations for children's inconvenient behaviour that might even be harmful for a child to hear. If you are up for recognizing them in yourself, you have already made a start on the repair:

'They're just doing that for attention'

Everyone needs attention, whatever age they are. If a child automatically has enough attention and feels secure that attention is there when they need it, they don't have to develop maladaptive ways to get it. If it's true that your child is doing something inconvenient to get attention, ask them instead to ask for some attention.

My daughter used to ask me for an apple that she didn't really want. What she wanted was me looking pleased and beaming at her. When I noticed the apples I gave her mostly went uneaten I twigged and asked her to ask for attention instead. This became a fun game between us and wasted far fewer apples. And she wasn't shamed for wanting what we all want at times – attention.

'They're being manipulative'

Toddlers don't have the skills to practise malice aforethought; they are just being themselves rather than planning to annoy you. Babies and children are their feelings; they haven't yet learned to observe their feelings, to work out what they want then ask for it. They need help with that.

When your child has a screaming fit, with kicking and perhaps head-banging, they are not carrying out a pre-planned strategy, they are being their feelings and need help to articulate them more conveniently. It will come in time.

If you feel an older child is trying to play you and their tantrum seems more like amateur dramatics than an actual tantrum, you can say how you experience their behaviour and put into words what they may be trying to tell you. For example: 'I feel like you are trying to trick me into letting you off your homework. I guess it can feel lonely doing it by yourself. I'll sit next to you while you do it instead.'

'They know just how to wind me up'

Just because you find your child's reaction to frustration unpleasant it doesn't mean they have any idea of the impact it's having or how to calculate how to achieve that impact. My daughter was not trying to wind me up when she sat on a step on the way back from the shops, even though I felt momentarily frustrated by it. Nor was she trying to wind up her father when she plonked herself on the floor at the swimming pool; she simply did not yet have the words to say what she wanted. Children learn the skill of using vocabulary to describe how they feel and what they want when we model this for them. And think about it: learning this skill is way more complicated than, say, learning to ask for a biscuit, especially when strong emotions are involved.

'They have something wrong with them'

Some children learn social skills more slowly than others, some have more difficulties dealing with frustration, some take longer to learn how to be flexible and problem-solve. This gives rise to some problems for them and for you. Most people probably think that plonking yourself down and screaming if you have to use the stairs instead of the lift is age appropriate for a toddler, but by the age of six or seven? The expectation is usually that your child should have grown out of it. But some children need more help in working out what it is they are feeling and finding appropriate ways to express or hold the feelings. What really helps is if they are expressed accurately, by someone on their side: you.

You will not always be able to fathom out what is going on, but being kind rather than punitive towards them in their distress will encourage future cooperation and nurture your relationship with them rather than hinder it.

If you need help or reassurance about your child's behaviour because it seems stuck at a stage for much longer than all their peers, see a family therapist or a social worker. Your doctor or the school should be able to guide you towards the help you need. It may lead to a diagnosis, which may feel like a relief to you and lead you to get more help and support.

The downside of a diagnosis is that it's like a judgement, a full stop. This means it can close a door on looking at and learning to understand the feelings behind a behaviour. A diagnosis can become an excuse for the behaviour. And there is a danger with a label that you can think things will never get any better and you lose your optimism around it.

Or worse, a situation that does not need to be might become medicalized. Let's look at ADHD. Think about this: more children born in August are diagnosed with ADHD than those born in September. I believe this shows that authorities tend to decide that those born in August have a disorder rather than merely being less mature than their peers who were born nearly a year earlier. This isn't to say all medicine designed to inhibit behaviour is bad, only that it should be a very last resort.

If you feel you cannot cope with your child's behaviour, seek professional help sooner rather than later, as the longer we have habits that are not helping our relationship with our child, the longer it can take to untangle them.

How strict should a parent be?

The three main approaches to trying to steer a child's behaviour tend to be: 1. being strict, 2. being lax and 3. collaborating.

1. Being strict is probably the most common way we may think about child discipline. It's about imposing your adult will upon the child. For example, you insist that your child tidies their room and you punish them if they don't.

Nobody is especially keen on having someone else's will imposed upon them and children are no exception. Some children may be compliant, but by no means all. This way of going about things leads to stand-offs, to winning and losing, to humiliation and anger.

The danger here is that what you're modelling is 'being right', 'being inflexible' and having a low tolerance for frustration yourself. By imposing your insistence on your child, you could be inadvertently teaching them they must be always right, inflexible and intolerant.

Then, you can get into a cycle of reciprocal inflexibility or, to put it another way, stand-offs and screaming matches or a withdrawal from communicating with you. This isn't a good long-term strategy for a relaxed relationship with your child. That's not to say you don't occasionally say, 'Toys away, right now!' but this needs to be an exceptional style of communication, not the usual one.

If being authoritarian is your go-to way of being with your children, you are also risking their future relationship with authority. It may block them from being able to cooperate with authority or being able to be a leader themselves or you may breed a dictator. To sum up: consistently imposing your will on your child is neither the best way to nurture morality or cooperation, nor is it a good way to have a good relationship with them.

2. Being lax is when you never communicate any standards or expectations to your child. Quite often when parents do not

have any boundaries for their children it is a backlash against anxiety-driven, risk-averse child-rearing or a reaction to their own authoritarian upbringing. Some children may be able to establish their own standards and expectations for themselves, but not all can. A child who does not know what is expected of them may feel lost and unsafe. Sometimes, when we parents are so determined not to do what our own authoritarian parents did, we can swing too far in another direction and not give our children any boundaries at all. If you think about it, in those situations we are still behaving more in reaction to our own parents than to the situation we are faced with in the present.

However, being lax is not all bad; it may sometimes be the best solution for a situation in the present. Because sometimes it is sensible to drop an expectation you had for your child because they are not ready for it. For example, your eldest might have found tidying up easy but your next child feels overwhelmed by it, so rather than have a battle, and one in which there will be no winners and there will be an erosion of goodwill, if a child is not ready for what you want them to be able to do eventually, drop the expectation for now. This means not insisting that the toys are tidied at all. This is not necessarily giving in but intentionally deciding to put off putting down a boundary for your child until they are ready for it. Being lax can be a positive short-term solution, until your child is ready for the collaborative method.

3. The collaborative method is when you and your child put your heads together to solve a problem so you're more of a counsellor than a dictator. This is my favourite approach as it's about trying to find a solution to the problem together.

So, what is the collaborative method, and how does it work?

1. Define the problem by defining yourself. 'I need your room to be tidy and I would like you to tidy it.'
2. Find out the feelings behind the behaviour. The child may need help with this. For example, 'Do you feel it's

unfair to have to tidy your room when your friend
made the mess?' 'Do you feel overwhelmed by the job
and feel it will take forever to sort out?'

3. Validate those feelings. 'I can understand that it feels
   unfair.' Or 'The beginning of a big job can feel
   overwhelming.'

4. Brainstorm solutions. 'I still need the room to be tidy.
   What would be the easiest way for you to do this?'

5. Follow through, repeating any steps as necessary.

And don't judge your child.

Stage 2 can be tricky, as it can feel hard saying something you
don't feel you want to endorse, but by *not* acknowledging a feeling you may think is inconvenient, your child is more rather than
less likely to dig in their heels. Because your child may not be
able to articulate everything they feel, you may have to use a
multiple-choice approach to find out the feelings behind the
problem, as in the above example.

When you have nailed down their feelings, then you can re-
define the problem, which is not 'Your room's a mess and you'd
better tidy it up or I'll throw away all your toys.' That would only
shame and threaten and build up resentment. Instead, empathize. This takes practice and can feel counter-intuitive, but how
children learn to consider other people's feelings is by having
their own considered.

When you brainstorm solutions together, it's important to
give your child the lead and not to dismiss out of hand anything
they suggest. So, they might come up with, 'We could leave my
room as it is.' Consider this: 'Yes, we could do that. You might be
happy with that solution, but I have difficulty with it. Not only
does it make me feel uncomfortable, but I'd find it hard to clean
the room or put away your clean clothes. What else could we
do?' 'I don't know.' 'It's okay. We're not in a rush, take your time.'
It's important not to be the clever one with all the answers

because, if you are, you disempower your child. 'I could put away the toys now, then have a break and then you could help me with the clothes because I find folding difficult.' 'Okay, that sounds good to me. Come and get me when it's time to start folding and we can work out ways of doing it.'

If you have been brought up with the authoritarian method, you may think it's the ideal. In that case, the collaborative method may seem very long-winded. However, the important thing here is that, as well as the room getting tidied, you are both being open about how you feel and therefore looking after your relationship and learning how to compromise and problem-solve. The real work of parenting is not the tidying, it is being with your children and helping them to develop. The collaborative method helps to develop the essential skills for socialized behaviour, which are: tolerance for frustration, flexibility, problem-solving skills and empathy.

More on tantrums

If you observe any child having a tantrum, they are not enjoying it. They are not doing it because they want to do it. It is unlikely to be a premeditated tactic on their part; they are being their feelings, their frustration, their anger and their sadness.

The same is true for tantrums as for any behaviour you don't like: ask yourself, what feelings is this communicating? What are the feelings behind the behaviour? Once you have guessed or worked it out, meet and validate those feelings. For example, 'You are very angry I cannot allow you ice cream before lunch.' And finally, once calm is restored, talk to the child to help them find a more acceptable way of expressing their feelings. 'You can tell me you are angry when I won't let you have what you want. It is easier for me to hear than when you are screaming.'

For example, a toddler's tantrum might be down to frustration. The toddler won't have chosen to have a tantrum, they'll just be having one. Once they are in the middle of it, they may even forget what it was that was frustrating them. The forbidden ice cream will be forgotten; they'll just be being their feeling. What I prefer is when they are not left to scream it out alone but if the caregiver stays in dialogue with them. Even if it is just, when they stop for breath, a sympathetic 'Oh dear, poor old you,' this means that on some level the child knows they are not alone with it. No one likes being left to dance alone, even if it is a dance of war. The exception may be when you, from your child's point of view, are deliberately misunderstanding them and this is therefore the cause of their anger, or you cannot contain your own feelings. However, I am uncomfortable at the thought of a child going through any extreme distress alone.

It does help to name the feeling behind the tantrum: 'You are really angry, aren't you?' If they are upset, they need comfort: 'I'm sorry you feel so sad.' This is not necessarily the same as giving them what they want, because that might not be possible or desirable. They might be crying because they cannot fly to the moon or swim with sharks.

What you can do is try to see the situation from the child's point of view, to comfort them because they cannot have what they want rather than punishing them or telling them off for wanting something you aren't going to or can't provide. A child will learn to contain their feelings by having them contained for them by someone else, someone who understands, who can stay calm, who doesn't shame them for feeling and acting like this, and for whom their feelings can never be too much or too big. Of course, that someone is you.

I think sometimes parents fear the tantrum too much and do not put down a boundary because they fear it may cause one. I am thinking of those parents I see carrying a child in one arm and heavy bags and a scooter in the other. Personally, I would rather comfort a child through a tantrum than carry a scooter around all day, but we all have different limits, so maybe I should mind my own business.

No one was ever healed by being made to feel ashamed or silly. You can contain your child when they are having a meltdown by holding them, and sometimes by staying close, getting down to their level and showing your concern for how they feel without becoming overwhelmed yourself. You can use words to help to validate how they are feeling, or maybe just loving gestures or looks.

Sometimes it may be necessary to remove the child from a situation, for example if they are a danger to themselves or others, or if they are disturbing other people. Then you say, 'I'm going to have to pick you up and take you out because I can't let you hurt the dog/disturb other people.' And then follow through.

What makes a tantrum worse is if you retaliate by shouting back or handling your child roughly. This is, effectively, punishing your child for having feelings. Ignoring a child having a tantrum is also a form of retaliation. Stop pushing the pushchair with the sobbing child in it, make sympathetic noises face to face with the little person in it and maybe pick them up for a cuddle.

It's not that you do what the child wants when they have a tantrum but that you are sympathetic to their frustration. What I used to do is verbalize what was happening. 'Oh, you are angry that I won't carry your scooter for you' (or whatever the trouble seems to be). Sooner or later your child's tolerance for frustration will begin to develop. I can remember the joy I felt when, after what seemed a very long time of me verbalizing what I thought my child was feeling every time she was in meltdown or close to it, she began to process her feelings into words for herself. 'I'm getting angry,' she'd say, and I'd inwardly marvel at how far we had come.

If you find yourself pushed to your limit because of your

child's tantrum, remember to reflect rather than react. And remember not to take a tantrum personally. Breathe, and stay in contact with yourself and with your child.

As you keep observing your child and noticing their moods, and experimenting and verbalizing to find out what your child is communicating, you will begin to learn their triggers for losing control of their feelings and behaviour and you'll be able to ward off a tantrum before it happens. A lot of parents know when it is time for their child to withdraw from a group, for example, to have some quiet time with a parent. Or when constraint in a pushchair is getting too much for them and they need the freedom to run about. Or when it is time for a meal before hunger takes a hold.

If your child frequently has tantrums yet is past the toddler stage, or if you find yourself getting into arguments, stand-offs and meltdowns with your child, it is a good time to think about what might be going wrong and what you could do differently.

No child is in permanent meltdown, so your first task is to make a note as to the where, when, with whom, what and why of the altercation to notice what the triggers are.

If the triggers are things like overstimulation or too much noise, you can take steps to avoid or limit those situations. It might be transitions – for example, when you ask the child to stop playing and come to the table. Or you may notice the problem can be when you are more impatient. Quite often, the problem is that we have put too high an expectation on the child. I'm not saying we shouldn't have high expectations of our children, but if we impose them before they are ready for them we are only going to frustrate them and ourselves. We all develop at different speeds.

The next job, after you've identified triggers, is to look at your role in the meltdown, or the other adult's role if it happens away from you, for example at school. Are you being inflexible? Often when a child communicates with us using behaviour – because they haven't learned to articulate their feelings yet – instead of considering the meaning of that behaviour, we make the mistake of thinking we must be stricter. Now this may 'work' with some children. And it is good to put down boundaries before you reach your limit and to be reasonably consistent with those boundaries, but sometimes you can go too far and become inflexible. This in turn sets an example of being stubborn to our children, or it simply frustrates them further and causes the situation to escalate. For example, if a child isn't getting the results expected of them at school, it might seem natural for the teachers and adults to think they need to spend longer on their allotted tasks and forego their break time. But if you observe that child, you might see that they are fidgeting, they are finding it hard to keep still, they cannot concentrate. Forcing them to sit still longer makes them worse, not better. It is a rare six-year-old who knows themselves so well that they can tell you, 'I have an excess of physical energy. I really need to run around outside before it is easy for me to sit still.' You will need to observe them to work this out.

At Eagle Mountain Elementary School in Fort Worth, Texas, teachers experimented with extending the children's break time to one hour – more than twice as long as they had previously. The teachers claim the children are now learning more. They have noticed the students now follow directions better, attempt to learn more independently and show more initiative in solving problems on their own. There has even been a drop in disciplinary issues. Parents have stated that their children are more creative at home and more social. This is just one example to show that clamping down on children is rarely the answer but opening up to them, seeing their needs and wants from their perspective, often is.

Reasoning – playing fact tennis – is very rarely a way to get a child to cooperate or to stop crying. Very young children cannot take in reasons. Feeling with them, on the other hand, frequently is. Parents rarely look to themselves when they feel irritated with their children. In their minds, the child is just being annoying and 'behaving badly'. But any situation between you and your child happens in relationship with them. It is co-created. And when we think of it like that, we do have a bearing on how they behave. It is easier to see the part we are playing when we let go of having to be right, winning and losing, and think more instead about how we can model cooperation and collaboration.

Whingeing

The behaviours that seem to particularly irk parents are: whining, whingeing, clinging and sobbing. That isn't the crying when kids fall over but the plaintive grizzling they do when parents can't think of a reason why their offspring might be sad or is still sad after the parent has made heroic efforts to distract them or cheer them up.

You may just want to get your child to stop when they do this; you may see it as 'bad' behaviour. But I wonder whether the irritation you feel at the whingeing is something to do with being shut off from what it felt like when you were an infant or a child and you felt sad and defenceless? The annoyance with your child could be coming from you not wanting to be taken back to the pain of re-experiencing old feelings of fragile vulnerability. So instead you try to shut down your child.

In addition, or alternatively, you may experience your child's whining or crying as a criticism of your parenting skills. Maybe you have an unspoken expectation that children should be happy all the time. Therefore, what to the child is just sadness or loneliness is felt by you as a reminder of your impotence over what your child is going through at that moment.

> Bella is a forty-five-year-old senior manager in a large corporation. She is married to Steve, a chef and restaurateur, and

they have three boys aged eight, twelve and fourteen. They are a lively family with plenty of weekend activities and socializing. The atmosphere at home is one of cheerful busyness. Bella and Steve both have demanding jobs and Juanita lives with them during the week as a childminder/housekeeper. She has been with the family since their oldest boy was five.

Bella thinks her youngest son, Felix, has a problem. 'Felix is really clingy,' she told me. 'Even though he's eight, he needs more attention, day and night, than my two other boys put together did when they were his age. I have wondered if I didn't bond properly with him as a baby, but I think I did. I really don't know why Felix seems so insecure.'

I was interested in why Bella had a low tolerance of Felix's clinging behaviour and what was perhaps stuck in their relationship. I told Bella to ask Felix about his dreams. I didn't expect to get any answers from his dreams, but I thought of it as a way of Felix talking and Bella listening.

Bella told me: 'Felix said he had a terrible dream where he was all alone and couldn't find anyone. I asked him if he'd ever experienced that in real life, confident he hadn't. I was surprised when he said he had. "I remember when we were visiting your brother in Wales, you left me alone in the car."

'As he said this, I remembered it too. My brother lives in the middle of nowhere and, once, when Felix was nearly two, he was asleep when we arrived so I got the other boys inside and unpacked the car and put the shopping away, then went back out to check on him. He'd woken up and was crying.

'I was devastated he'd remembered this. I said sorry, and "You couldn't have been alone in the car for more than five minutes, darling," and we had a hug. I began to wonder how one tiny incident from six years ago could still be around for him now.'

The incident may have been tiny for Bella, but it probably wasn't for Felix. I asked Bella if Felix had ever been left alone in a strange place, before or since. She said, 'No, but when he was little, twenty months, he had such a severe septic throat that he had to be hospitalized. The antibiotics didn't work and, for a week, he was put in a coma and on a machine to help him breathe. While in the coma, he was sometimes alone, but after he was taken out of it Steve or I were always with him.'

'Bella,' I said, 'how awful for you that your son was so sick he had to be put into a coma.' She replied, 'Oh, it was fine – I mean, not very nice, but you get through these things.'

When Bella said this I felt pushed away, that my concern was unwanted. And in that moment it felt to me as though she had been – and was still – pushing away her own feelings about Felix's illness. I felt shocked and moved myself, imagining what it must have been like for the little boy to be so ill and what it must have been like to be his parents. Bella said, 'Steve said we might have lost him, but I couldn't go there.' I felt another wave of sadness and told her so. As I looked at her I noticed that she too had tears in her eyes.

I said, 'This could be why Felix is clingy – because he had to cling on to life. Although he couldn't have known consciously you weren't there when he was in a coma, it's possible he knew it on another level, which perhaps explains his dream of being alone.'

Whether this was true or not, it resonated with Bella, helped make sense of Felix's behaviour for her. And this in turn made it easier for her to empathize with Felix.

Another thing that may have happened is that Bella finally allowed herself to feel the fear and sadness about losing Felix that she'd repressed for so long. It's completely normal to want to lock away our difficult feelings, but when we do we risk becoming insensitive to the difficult feelings of others, including our children. All the time Bella was repressing her feelings about Felix's illness, Felix's feelings irritated her.

When Bella did finally allow herself to experience what nearly losing Felix had felt like, it didn't completely consume her, as she'd feared. 'Before, I always thought it was Felix's fault he was clingy. I'd think, your brothers are fine, so why aren't you? I realize now that you can't blame anyone for their feelings.'

After we talked it was Bella who had a dream – in fact, a nightmare. She dreamed two of her nieces and Felix went swimming in the sea and got into difficulties. The girls were saved but Felix drowned. Bella woke up with a start, tearful and upset, and went to check on Felix, who was asleep, safe and sound. The irony of this action struck her – it was usually Felix coming into his parents' bedroom.

These days, if Bella does feel irritated with Felix, she takes responsibility for this. She's not sure this is down to Felix being less clingy, whether she has softened towards his clinginess, whether she's reaching out more towards him, or all three.

There are as many reasons for clinginess and whingeing as there are children and relationships with each of their caregivers. The reason why I put in the above case study was not because a child having nearly died is a common reason for clinginess. It's because not wanting to be sensitive to the feelings our children trigger in us causes us to get stuck in our relationships with our children, prevents us being as close as we might want to be and so reduces our children's capacity for happiness.

Acknowledging and validating feelings – our own and our children's – is important, not only for our own and their mental health but as a way of understanding our triggers, our children's triggers and for gaining a deeper knowledge of why we all behave how we do.

All feelings – clinginess, ghosts in the wardrobe, monsters under the bed, just feeling sad or overwhelming frustration – make sense once we find their context. If the context isn't obvious, it doesn't mean there isn't one. The first step is to accept the child's feeling, which will help you understand their behaviour. Once this happens, you will be able to tolerate it and so be in a better position to collaborate with your child to come up with solutions to make helpful changes.

Parental lying

Sometimes, families have secrets which are in fact lies. You may not even think of it like that; you may think it's just withholding information the child doesn't need or which may even harm them.

But when a family withholds information or there are lies within the family, even if family members are not consciously aware of the truth of the situation, it will have an impact. That's because, in our bodies, we can feel if something is not straightforward and in the open.

If you're telling lies – or omitting information – to protect children from the reality of a situation what you are doing is dulling their instincts. You are telling them something different from what they will be sensing and feeling. It won't feel comfortable for them and, if they can't articulate that discomfort, it's likely to surface in inconvenient behaviour.

This case study was used in my training as a psychotherapist to teach us about this phenomenon.

Mr and Mrs X went to see a psychotherapist, Dr F, about their teenage son A. A's behaviour, said his parents, was out of control. He was playing truant from school, using drugs and alcohol, was sullen and uncommunicative and had been stealing from his mother's bag. What they wanted from the therapist was advice on how to get him to toe the line.

Dr F explained to them that when a child reaches adolescence they feel a need to separate from their parents, to form or come together with their own new tribe. When they feel they have established a separate identity from their parents, they don't need to push away so much and things settle down. The Xs insisted that their son's behaviour went beyond this.

Dr F asked for a history of A's early life. The way the Xs described what a happy, normal little boy A had been sounded stilted, bland and without details. The Xs glanced at each other, as if they were communicating something secret. Dr F noticed this. He said, 'What are you not telling me?' The Xs fell silent and looked at each other again.

'Have you two always got on well?' Dr F prompted. 'We weren't together then,' said Mr X at last. His wife shot him a stern look. 'You split up when he was little?' Then it came out. Mr X wasn't A's father but, as far as A was concerned, he was. A's real father, said Mrs X, had been 'no good'. He had womanized, was an alcoholic and, when A was eighteen months old, he'd died in a car accident caused by him drink driving.

'A wouldn't remember him. He was hardly ever there anyway,' said Mrs X.

'He might not remember him knowingly, but in his body, he might have felt his presence and then the lack of his presence,' Dr F suggested.

'What we're worried about is that this type of behaviour is in his genes,' said Mr X. Behaviour, Dr F told them, is a communication; it has a meaning. 'So what is A's behaviour telling you?'

'It's like he's telling us to fuck off,' said Mr X.

'You have told A a lie, a huge lie. He doesn't know what it is, but he may feel that something doesn't add up and it disturbs him,' said Dr F.

'We haven't lied, we just haven't told him,' said the Xs.

'Lying by omission,' said Dr F.

'So, what should we do?' asked the Xs.

'I'm not going to tell you what to do. I'm thinking, though, that this could be part of the problem.'

The Xs decided to tell their son. He was furious. He found out his real father had a brother. He went to stay with the brother, started working hard, did well at school and got into university.

His parents had their wish that their son began to behave himself. All they had to do now was repair the rupture. This would mean understanding their son's anger, owning up to preferring a perfect picture of a perfect family rather than telling the truth, acknowledging the impact this had had on their son and apologizing and accepting whatever feelings their son had about it. I never learned whether this happened, as the story stopped there.

Quite often, when we'd prefer that something wasn't happening or hadn't happened, we lie by omission to our children. It is natural to want to protect our children from difficult feelings, but it is not their feelings that are a problem, it is our being terrified of their feelings that's the problem. So I believe it would be better if they were informed, for example, that you or your partner were having difficulties and that you were working to solve them and hoped that you would, rather than keeping matters that do affect your child's world a secret. If they are worried, you can soothe them. If we do not tell such bad news in a form a child can handle, they will sense the atmosphere anyway and may come up with even worse explanations for it.

I don't believe it's good for children to be lied to, or lied to by omission, so I don't advocate holding back on bad news, such as the death of someone important to the family. But it needs to be given with the reassurance that, although we feel desperately sad now, and although we will not forget the person, we will get used to their loss and life will carry on and be enjoyed again. In the same way, if one parent who had hitherto lived in the family home is moving out of it, this needs to be talked about before it happens and the children need to know the plans and proposed routine of how they are going to keep their world together – in other words, still see enough of both parents in a regular and predictable way.

There is probably an age-appropriate way of communicating anything. For example, you can tell a child: 'I am unwell, I'm going to the doctor and, with a bit of luck, I will get better. I'm sorry if I seem distracted. I'm worried about my illness.' This is better than keeping your cancer a secret. If your child is adopted, it is best to tell them in an age-appropriate way from the start so they always know and never have the shock of finding out.

We cannot protect children from the inevitable bereavements and calamities that life will throw at us and at them, but we can be alongside them and feel with them and help to contain their feelings when, inevitably, calamities happen.

All children need the reassurance that they matter, that they are wanted and loved, not just in occasional words but by being shown the love, in how your face lights up when you see them, in the give and take of your interactions, by being included in your life, and by parents allowing themselves the leisure to enjoy their children and enjoy being with them. It is difficult to do this fully if you are holding some information back that affects them. They have a right to know it.

Children's lies

I was at a welcome talk for new parents at my daughter's secondary school and the headteacher, Margaret Connell, looked at all of us parents and gave it to us straight. She said, 'Your child will lie to you.' I thought, 'Oh, not my daughter, we have a great relationship.' She went on, 'Even if you think your daughter tells you everything, she will lie to you as she enters adolescence, and your job,' she told us, 'is not to make a stonking big deal of it.'

When I asked Margaret about this years later she told me this: 'Everybody lies. Of all the bad things we do, lying is the most common and the one we think least about. But, for some reason, parents seem to put this sin above all sins. If the child has done something they shouldn't have, maybe something relatively trivial, and she says she didn't do it, the parents then say, "I know my daughter, she has her faults, but she wouldn't lie." And the problem is, this puts the child into a corner and it means, whatever the matter is, you never reach an end of it.'

All children lie; all adults lie too. It's great when we don't, because it gives us a better chance to have proper dialogue and real intimacy. But we all do it and we shouldn't treat our children like the greatest sinners when they do too.

After all, we give our children very mixed messages about lying and when it's acceptable in our culture. We tell them not to lie, but then we also tell them to pretend to be grateful for an ugly scarf Granny has knitted them for Christmas for the third year running. If you think about it, children have to learn a complicated lesson about when it is appropriate to lie.

Children witness their parents telling lies all the time. They'll have overheard you ask your partner, for example, to tell his colleagues you can't come to the work reception when the correct version is that you don't want to go. There is no reason for your children to believe you will never lie to them if they have witnessed you behaving like this, with perfect power to persuade other people that the truth is other than it is.

If you think about lying, it is an accomplished thing for a child to do. Firstly, they have to conceive of an alternative reality and say, 'This happened.' Then they must keep that in their mind along with what really happened. And they must distinguish between both in order to properly lie and then – and this is the really clever bit – they also have to bear in mind what you are thinking and what you know.

A toddler may indulge in deceitful behaviour, like feeding the dog behind your back with something they don't fancy eating, but they don't really begin to lie in the way I described above until they reach the age of about four. Then they feel that they've got a new superpower. 'Wow, I can make stuff up and people will believe me! This is amazing!'

Quite often, children lie because the adults in their life would not be calm and unjudgemental about the truth. Some children tell lies to get out of trouble, others are fantasy lies or lies to please grown-ups or to do others a good turn.

Sometimes children tell a lie to tell an emotional truth. When they are asked what's wrong and they do not know how to explain, they invent a narrative to fit their feelings.

One day at nursery school when Flo was aged three, she did not seem her usual bouncy self. The teacher asked her if anything was wrong. She replied, 'My goldfish has died.' At pick-up, the teacher told me about that conversation and I said, 'Er, but we have never had a goldfish.'

Thinking about it, I realized she was telling a kind of truth. My beloved aunt had died, and I had naturally been upset about this. Flo would have seen me cry; maybe I was not as interested in what she was absorbed by; maybe I didn't hear when she talked to me; and generally, although I was there physically, I was not as available and present with her. Maybe she was missing what I was normally like to the value of one goldfish? Or, more likely, she could handle and conceive of the death of a goldfish, but this massive, terrible thing of my bereavement needed to be reduced to the value of one goldfish for her to be able to handle it. I told the teacher what I thought had really happened.

It can be easier for a child to hold on to a fantasy than to handle the truth, and we need to respect that. The more we continue to put our feelings, and our children's feelings, into words, the less they will have to lie to get their emotional truth across to us. This takes years to learn.

Sometimes their fantasy lie is a form of self-soothing and we must, as with all aberrant behaviour, look to understand the feelings behind the behaviour rather than condemn the child for committing it. If they cannot take in the enormity of it, like my daughter could not take in my aunt's death, they will break it down into a goldfish or whatever their equivalent is.

And there are yet more reasons your older child will lie. As you may have predicted, Miss Connell's wise words came true and Flo did lie to me, when she was fifteen. When I found out, I remembered Miss Connell's words and did not treat this as the greatest tragedy ever to descend upon me.

Instead, I listened to my daughter's explanation. She and a friend each told their parents that they were revising at the other's house but instead they went to the local university's student union bar.

I really listened when she said that she had to lie because I would never have let her go there! That much was true, I told her, I wouldn't have – because it was illegal: she was not only under age to drink, it was a private bar which they weren't entitled to use.

But, I said, the real reason I wouldn't have allowed her to go there was because I was scared. I was scared because, when I was fifteen, I had similar adventures and didn't tell my parents about them. And, looking back on my own escapades, I did put myself in danger and was just lucky I got away with it.

I told her I wasn't yet ready to let her put herself in the sort of danger I'd put myself in at her age, drinking too much and trying to impress people who were older and who I saw as more sophisticated than I was, of losing my head in the moment. I told her she'd have to wait until I felt confident to allow her to do things like that, and I said I could understand if she felt frustrated by that. Indeed, the following year I did feel confident enough to give her more freedom. When Flo was sixteen I let her camp at a pop festival with a group of her peers, and no harm came to any of them. We did have conversations before she went where I shared my fears: What are you going to do when your phone has died and you've lost your friends? How can you tell if an offered drug poses a risk? (A very cunning trick question on my part.) Her answers were sensible enough.

Now Flo is an adult she can enjoy scaring me with some of the things she omitted to mention at the time. Apparently, by 3 a.m., theirs was the only tent not on fire, so she and her friend left the site, walked miles to the train station and slept there. A marvellous adventure for a pair of sixteen-year-olds. Flo felt she couldn't tell me at the time because she enjoyed having that secret for a while.

It's better if you don't overreact to what your child does and tells you, as not overreacting makes it more likely that you will keep the lines of communication open. I had perhaps erred by overreacting with my fears, veering too far from the ideal of containment, which is why she deemed me unready to hear this story until years later.

When parenting a teenager, remember what it was like to be a teenager yourself, straining at the restrictions your parents put in place to try to stop their fears coming true. Adolescents do need to keep some things, like that relatively harmless tale of my daughter's, private. They need this privacy in order to forge their separate identity. Teenagers may also lie, or lie by omission, to create space for themselves. It isn't that they are necessarily up to something tremendously bad; they're up to something that they may want to keep for themselves or in their friendship group because they are separating from the tribe of family and parents and forming their own new tribe.

What you're aiming for is to keep those lines of communication open from babyhood to adulthood. It's important that children feel they can tell you the truth, that all their feelings will be accepted, even – or rather, especially – those feelings and attitudes you find inconvenient. If you are not a safe person to talk to, who can they turn to when, for example, they are being bullied at school, or feel spooked by the sexual overtones of their judo instructor? You need to contain a child's feelings and not overreact to what they show or tell you by not being judgemental and by getting them to brainstorm possible solutions to problems rather than immediately telling them what they should be doing. We have been around longer than them, and sometimes when they tell us something it is tempting to tell them what they should do, but, if possible, hold back, so that you instil confidence in your child rather than disempowering them. If you are a sounding board rather than always an oracle, your child is more likely to keep telling you the truth.

If a child lies – or engages in any other behaviour you'd rather change – instead of reacting, look to the reasons and feelings behind the lie or the behaviour. If you understand and validate those feelings, you give them a chance to find more acceptable ways of expressing themselves and their needs.

Margaret Connell told me about a pupil of hers. 'I had a pupil once who, whenever there was a disaster in the world, she had a relation in it. Whether it was an earthquake or a train crash, she had a second cousin or a brother-in-law or a family friend in it. After a while it dawned on me that this was not entirely likely, and that she was driven to lie to get attention and get sympathy, probably because she couldn't or hadn't been allowed to ask for attention and sympathy in a straightforward way. So she invented these unlikely scenarios based on whatever that day's news was.'

To get to the root of the problem, it is important to go beyond the lies and find out what is lacking in that child's life, or what is happening, or has happened, to them that they need such sympathy and attention. And also what is happening that they have to take such a roundabout route to secure it.

You may think, yes, but lying is still wrong. But having a stern, moralistic approach towards lying does not make children more truthful. In fact, research shows that it makes children more accomplished at lying.

Researcher Victoria Talwar visited two schools in West Africa with similar pupil intakes but very different disciplinary regimes. One was roughly equivalent to a typical Western school: if you did something wrong, maybe lied or didn't do your work very well, you would get guidance about how to act next time in a chat with a teacher and perhaps a detention. The other school was punitive: the children were taken out and beaten for misdemeanours.

Talwar was interested to see which regime would be better at raising a truthful child so she did an experiment with the children called the peeping game. She invited a child into the room and said, 'You sit here, facing the wall. I'm going to bring out three objects behind you. You have to guess from the noise it makes what each object is.' With the third object, she played a trick and gave it a completely different noise, for example the noise of a greetings-card birthday tune when the object was a football.

Before she asked for the child's answer, she said, 'I've just got to pop out of the room for a moment. Don't peek!' When she came back, she said, 'You didn't peek, did you?' The child invariably replied, 'No.' Then she asked, 'What was the third object? Could you guess from the noise?' The child almost always said, 'It's a football.' Because they had peeked. They almost all peeked.

Talwar then asked, 'How did you know that? Did you peek?' And at that point she could measure how much and how effectively the children lied. In the school with the not-so-strict regime, some children lied, some didn't; it was around the same ratio she'd found when she did the test in other countries. But the children in the school with the punitive regime were all incredibly quick to lie, and they all lied very convincingly.

So, unwittingly, by cracking down hard on lying, the school had become a machine for turning out highly effective liars – something my daughter's headteacher, Margaret Connell, had known all along.

When your child lies – and I say 'when' and not 'if' – remember all the reasons for lying. It's a developmental stage, they are copying you, they are creating their own private space, they're lying to communicate a feeling, to avoid punishment or to avoid upset. If the lying is a problem, it's better to problem-solve and find out what's behind the lie rather than being punitive. That will only make your child into a better liar.

The more judgemental you are, the more punitive you are, the more you will stop your child confiding in you. They will still want to please you, to get your approval, but they will do it by putting aside honesty, by putting aside their real self, perhaps at the expense of their mental health. A draconian regime does not turn out good, moral citizens. Nor is it likely to help them have a mutually rewarding relationship with you, which in turn may jeopardize their ability to form sustaining, satisfying relationships in life.

Remember Margaret Connell's words: 'Your child will lie and your job is not to make a stonking big deal of it.'

Boundaries: define yourself and not the child

What children – and all of us – need is love plus boundaries, not one or the other.

Boundaries are important for any relationship. A boundary is the metaphorical line you draw in the sand that you won't allow the other to cross. Just beyond that line is your limit and, if your limit is crossed, that's when you lose your cool and cannot handle your frustration any longer.

That's why it's a good idea to put a boundary down before you reach your limit. One example of a boundary is saying something like, 'I cannot allow you to play with my keys,' and taking the keys away. A boundary is stated calmly but firmly. When you reach your limit, you have no such control and maybe you'll react in a way that frightens your child, maybe by grabbing back your keys and yelling at them.

Sometimes parents find it hard to set boundaries. For example, when a much-longed-for child arrives after many miscarriages, IVF, or even, in some tragic circumstances, after a death of another child. Parents can be so blinded by love by such a happy miracle that they do not know where their own limits are and revere their progeny like a god. Without boundaries, your child will not learn where your and other people's limits are, and if you grow up believing you are omnificent, you might go beyond good self-esteem into self-delusion. We all need boundaries so that we have some sort of structure to our lives that supports us and so we can learn to live together, and children are no exception. Get into the habit of putting down a boundary by describing yourself and not them, so it's 'I cannot allow you to have my keys' rather than 'I've told you before, you are not to be trusted with keys.' Even if your baby cannot understand words yet, defining yourself in this way is a good habit to get into. When you are later setting a boundary with a teenager, they'll be able to hear 'I need you back at ten for my sake' more easily than 'You are too young to be out after ten.'

This is from an email from a friend who I had just shared my define-yourself-not-the-child theory with.

> The other night, instead of saying my usual 'Go and brush your teeth. Go and brush! I've told you four times, I'm not going to tell you again, I'm going to take away some of your screen time if you don't do it now, and so on. I said 'I'm really tired tonight and I'm getting really, really tired of listening to my voice nagging on about your teeth. Can you please go and do them?' And he did. Love him.

You want your boundaries to be effective, so don't dish out empty threats. Before a child realizes that the threat is empty, it is too scary and therefore liable to shatter a child's thought processes rather than help them learn consideration. And, once they learn that your threats can be empty, they will not be able to take you seriously. So, mean what you say, do not relent and give them the keys back (or whatever it is). It may mean a tantrum, but you can be sympathetic about their frustration about not having the keys and still hold on to your keys – and your boundary.

With babies and toddlers you put boundaries in place by physically picking the child up and removing them from what you do not want them to do or disturb. This must be done respectfully. Respecting a child is not 'spoiling' them.

For example, you might say, 'I cannot let you tease the dog, so I'm going to pick you up and carry you away from the dog.' Even if your child has not learned to speak yet, your kind and firm tone and you physically removing them from what they are doing will gradually teach them that you disapprove of the activity they were engaged in.

Or it might be: 'I carried you out of the room because you cannot make a noise when someone is making a speech.' They might not understand what you say, but they will begin to learn on an embodied level what is and what isn't appropriate. If a child is using a toy keyboard as a weapon, you might show them and tell them that keyboards are for playing on, not for hitting with or throwing. Then you might say, 'Unless you play on the keyboard instead of hitting with it, I will have to take it away.' And then, if the inappropriate behaviour continues, you take it away.

Speak calmly, kindly and firmly, do what you said you would do and be consistent. The advantage of not issuing empty threats, of following through with a physical removal, is that your child really does learn to take you seriously. You are a person who means what they say. What surprised me about using this approach was that, by the time the child grows too big for you to be able to physically remove them from the situation, they have learned that you mean what you say, and so they do as instructed, as if you could still pick them up. If you are past the being-able-to-pick-them-up stage, it is important to put down boundaries by defining yourself, not defining them and not getting into reason wars (see below, pp. 216–18). Remember: you are both on the same side. You both want them and you to be content. The way to achieve this is to listen and empathize with their feelings, to contain their frustration and to learn when to be firm (when your own limit is being approached, or when their safety is at stake, or, more usually, when your fears about their safety are more than you can tolerate) and when to be flexible. You can be flexible when, for example, a change in plans or expectations won't jeopardize anything in the long run, when you are being firm for the sake of keeping up appearances, when you are veering towards manipulating rather than relating with your child. As I was typing this, I was listening with one ear to some children playing in a neighbour's garden. They were getting more and more boisterous and began to sound as though they were on the edge of hysteria. Then I heard an adult address them: 'I am finding your noise too much for me. You can either play quietly out here or you will have to come in.' I loved her firm yet calm voice and I felt safer, as though I had been one of those children who was losing control and needed a boundary. After a while they got noisier again and she came out and said in a firmer voice, 'Right, inside now,' and in they all trooped. They knew she meant it.

Framing your boundaries with as little negativity as possible also helps. So instead of 'Don't paint on the walls,' say, 'Walls are not for painting on, paper is for painting on. Here is some paper.' In the following example of a repair after a rupture, Aoife's mum, Gina, learned to do just this with her toddler.

We just had a lovely moment. Aoife was washing her hands after painting and she filled a bowl with water and put it really carefully on the side. I said, 'You were so careful then, Aoife' and she said, 'Yes, I was' – then she hugged me. I realized instead of being positive, I'm usually saying, 'Don't spill the water,' 'Don't make the floor wet.' Her hug was my reward for my good parenting behaviour.

At first, boundaries are about keeping your child safe. We might say, 'Play in the garden, not the road, as the road is not safe.' Then they are about considering the environment and other people. Often, when parents put down a boundary, we pretend it is not about defining ourselves. We say things like, 'You've got to turn off the television at the end of this programme because you've watched too much.' By doing that, you are defining the child. No one likes to be defined or told what they need when they don't think they need it. In this case, what you really mean is 'I don't want the television on any more so I will be turning it off after this.' It is not only okay to self-define rather than pretend to them (and to yourself) that you are being objective, it is good modelling for them. You are showing them that you are listening to your feelings, working out what you want from what you feel, then you are going for it. This is key to staying sane.

You may have read that it's not good for children to have more than one hour's screen time a day so you might feel you are stating an objective fact when you tell them they've watched too much and so they must turn it off. But it might not feel like too much to them, so you may be inviting an unwelcome game of fact tennis. So, define yourself, give your boundary with an I-statement, say how you feel: 'I am not comfortable with you watching any more television, so I am switching it off after the end of this programme. Would you like to play something else, or help me cook the supper?'

Losing your temper with your child can traumatize them and

close them down. So it's much better to know your limits and to be firm about a boundary before you get to that limit. The boundary is when you stop the behaviour, and the limit is when you blow a fuse if the boundary has not been put down.

So, if you lose your cool after overhearing two hours of YouTube memes or cartoons, two hours is your limit, so you need to set the boundary before two hours. Boundaries benefit the person we give them to but they are also for the benefit of the person laying down the boundary, and we should not pretend otherwise.

If you pretend that you have worthy reasons for a boundary, you are teaching your children to hide their real feelings behind worthy reasons. This will make communication with them more difficult, as they will get good at the game of inventing worthy reasons rather than sharing how they feel. Having the more difficult parenting conversations – about sex and porn, about social media, about stress and pressures and feelings – will be much harder unless your habit from the start has been clear communication and you're in the habit of talking about your own feelings and listening to their feelings and taking them seriously.

If you make up reasons for boundaries, even when they sound reasonable you will get into all sorts of difficulties. 'But Daddy lets me stay up until eight o'clock and you're saying I have to go to bed at seven thirty?' 'Who is right?' the child will wonder. The truth in such a situation might be: 'Daddy doesn't mind if you stay up until eight, and I do. And tonight I want you in bed by seven thirty because there is a programme I want to watch at eight, undisturbed.'

We owe our children honesty, so that means sharing our feelings with them rather than pretending we don't have any. Our feelings and personal preferences inevitably come into a decision like what time they should go to bed, and we must not pretend they don't.

Likewise, children may resent it if rules seem petty. In one family, their eldest child was autistic. He needed to know what was going to happen and when, and it had to happen then and it had to be the same every day. The parents brought up their subsequent two sons with the same routine and rules because they felt it would be 'unfair' if they allowed the younger children flexibility they hadn't allowed their first. 'John had to go to bed at eight when he was twelve, so you do too,' they'd say. If you are that inflexible and refuse to see each child as an individual, they may gradually store up resentment against you or against their sibling. And storing up resentment is storing up trouble.

The rule of thumb for setting a boundary is to define yourself and not the child. For example, suppose your child is playing music really loudly and it's disturbing you. They are absorbed and enjoying themselves. You, on the other hand, are beginning to feel resentful. In other words, you are approaching your limit. Define yourself, describing how you feel rather than defining your child. Say: 'I'm finding this music too loud. I would like you to turn it down, please,' rather than, 'Your music is too loud, turn it down, please.'

My parents never defined themselves when they gave me commands or put down boundaries, and I remember that it felt frustrating. I might not have been able to put my finger on why at the time, but something felt not quite real about it and it made me feel angry and lonely.

I decided that, when I had a child, I would do things differently. I would be honest. I would tell the truth. That's not to say it didn't feel like a risk to own my selfishness when I told my daughter I was cold and bored and that was why I wanted to leave the playground, but it turned out well. By modelling and saying how I felt and then saying what I wanted, my daughter learned to do the same thing. And we did not get into reason wars.

What is a reason war? A reason war is when you play fact tennis and pretend that feelings don't come into a decision at all, then it escalates to a war or stand-off. For example:

ADULT We have to go because we have to make lunch.
CHILD No, we don't. We can eat the leftovers.
ADULT It's time to go home for lunch now, anyway.
CHILD I'm not hungry, and there are apples in the bag, if
   you are.
ADULT You need a proper lunch and we're going home and
   that's that.
CHILD Whaaaaaaaaaaah!

If you often find yourself locked into battles like this, it's because
you've taught your child the rules of fact tennis. You might think
it's better or less selfish-sounding to give a reason that involves
them ('It's time for your lunch!'), but if it's not the real reason you
want to leave the playground – say, the real reason is that you want
your own lunch – you are giving them too much space to argue
with you. There's no arguing with you wanting your own lunch.

The way to get out of reason wars is to describe how you
feel and say what you want. It is easier to negotiate when everyone shares their feelings instead of pretending everything is
about a reason.

So, instead, try this approach:

ADULT We have to go now because I want my lunch.
CHILD I don't want to go.
ADULT I'm sorry you don't want to go, but I'll get grumpy if I
   don't have lunch. I'll give you two more minutes to finish
   your game and then we're going.

And then you follow through.

I remember being very pleasantly surprised one day when I
told my daughter I was getting cold and bored in the playground
so we'd be leaving in five minutes and she negotiated down on
my behalf, saying, 'We can go in two if you like!'

A child who is respected by being listened to and having their feelings taken seriously has less inclination to act out their frustrations and is more likely to want to get along with you and to learn how to empathize. A child who isn't listened to enough will be more demanding. With very young children, it takes many years until a small person can articulate themselves clearly so you'll need to listen by observing. Here is a case study to illustrate what I mean.

> My son, Paul, who is six, has speech and language difficulties that are probably related to autism, but we have had no formal diagnosis. When he was a baby and a toddler, the house sometimes felt like a war zone.
>
> Once my partner and I started trying to understand life from his perspective, all our lives got better. We had to put a lot of time and effort into watching and listening to learn from him. He taught us patience. What we learned is when we can nudge him a little further and when to back off. We also have a daughter, who is two years older than him. Because she is more like we are in the way she works, we didn't have to puzzle her out as much. But while we were learning about our son, we started to observe and listen better to our daughter too. Although she was always lovely to be around, we've noticed that, as we have become more considerate of her, she has become more considerate of us.

Setting boundaries with older children and teenagers

> '*When I was a boy of 14, my father was so ignorant I could hardly stand to have him around. But when I got to be 21, I was astonished at how much the old man had learned in seven years.*'
>
> – Mark Twain

It can feel much more difficult than it did when they were younger to set boundaries with teenagers. It is easier, though, if you are already in the habit of defining yourself rather than them. But if you are not, it is never too late to start.

> When my son Ethan was a teenager, things got serious. He'd had a few moments of getting into trouble at school – nothing out of the ordinary. But when he was nearly sixteen, things got bad. One day, I got a call to pick him up from the police station because he'd been involved in a 'supermarket sweep'. A group he's friendly with had filled a trolley in a supermarket with beer and sweets and tried to make a dash for it to steal the lot. He said he had no idea why he did it, he just got swept along with it all. This was totally out of character for him. But then again, I worried that it might be becoming his character . . .

Beer and sweets. This is a snapshot of where a teenager is at – halfway between childhood and adulthood. How are they supposed to cope with that? Can you remember how confusing it was for you? And how are we, as parents, supposed to cope with it? You can say how the behaviour makes you feel. 'Disappointed' is a word often used by their parents when children reach this stage. It stings more for the child when a parent defines themselves like this than when they try to define their teen by saying, for example, 'You're behaving like an idiot.' The other tool is to go through this problem-solving list, breaking it down so the teen can understand their thought process. By doing this, the teen will eventually start to be able to use it themselves.

1. Define the problem

In this instance: 'I don't find shoplifting acceptable. We are going to have to understand why this happened and work out how it can never happen again. I felt mortified when I had to pick you up from the police station.'

2. Find the feelings behind the problem

The conversation may go a bit like this: 'What happens when you five boys get together because, individually, you do not appear to be natural criminals?'
   'I don't know.'
   'Okay, take your time. How did you feel before you did it?'
   'We were joking and laughing.'
   'Then what happened?'
   'We started to dare each other.'
   'Then what happened?'
   'We just did it.'
   'I'm wondering whether the problem seems to be that when you five boys get together you egg each other on, get carried away and develop a peer pressure between you that is hard to resist. Is that it?'
   'Yeah.'

3. Brainstorming solutions

'So, next time this happens – when you're about to do something you know isn't a good idea – how are you going to put the brakes on so the situation doesn't get out of hand?'
   'I suppose we could just imagine it, rather than actually do it. Say how funny it'd be *if* we did it.'
   'That might still be a laugh, and without the terrible consequences.'
   'Yeah.'

Steps 2 and 3 may have to be repeated because there might be something else going on for the teen which they need to talk about, such as feeling they can't cope with what is expected of them at school, or any other problem. Perhaps you might say something like 'I'm wondering if you were already feeling angry and rebellious because you got a detention at school?' But remember: let them take the lead in the brainstorming.

You'll probably want to set a boundary for future behaviour. Set the boundary by defining yourself and not them.

So, rather than 'You cannot be trusted, you are grounded,' it's 'I am keeping you at home for a couple of weeks because, after picking you up from the police station, I am giving myself a break from worry. I want you close for a while.' Keep naming and sharing your own feelings.

Don't judge your child. Labelling them as incapable, impulsive, untrustworthy or immature will not help them improve. Boundaries are good, such as 'I'm not letting you out until I feel more confident to do so,' but a punitive stance increases stubbornness and goes no further in enhancing a deeper understanding between you. And keep the dialogue going. Follow through and check in to see how the solutions are working out.

Remember: when you want to put down a boundary, define yourself and not the teen. Give your own feelings as your reason – because it is your feelings that *are* the reason. For example, your thirteen-year-old wants to catch the night bus back across town on their own. You could say: 'You are right, you probably can catch that bus and know how to behave responsibly and safely on it. The trouble is, I am not yet ready to let you do it. I must get used to the idea that you are getting more adult and that you can look out for yourself. You are going to have to bear with me for a bit before I can let it happen.' By saying it like this, you are modelling honesty as well as putting down the boundary. Your teenage child will be able to hear that it's not because of anything to do with them that they are not allowed on public transport in the middle of the night but because of you. They would know this anyway, but by not pretending it is otherwise they may be able to be more tolerant of your decision and so it will help your relationship with them.

Teenagers and young adults

Although it's a cliché to say it, your teenage child is going through a stage. Human beings don't reach maturity until we're (roughly) in our mid-twenties. Until then we are more likely to make errors in risk-taking and decision-making. It's thought to be because our frontal lobes, where a lot of our thinking takes place, have not yet achieved fast connections to other parts of our brains. But, at the same time, our ability to feel excited is reaching a once-in-a-lifetime peak. Teenagers appear to feel things more deeply and completely than either younger children or adults. While impulsivity exercises their emotions, their capacity to say, 'That's a bad idea,' or 'Don't do that' has not yet caught up. Some people develop impulse control later than others, but this doesn't mean they'll never learn to look ahead at likely outcomes before they act. Most people get there in the end.

Just like the stage your child went through when they were a toddler discovering their autonomy, teens need love plus boundaries and a heavy dose of parental optimism that they will master their emotions and their impulsivity. Remember: behaviour is at its most challenging just before a new behavioural milestone is reached. Think of it in terms of them experiencing emotion in colour whereas, in comparison, we are experiencing it only in black and white. It's great if they can channel all this emotional energy into creativity, like music, or into sports, but it is not unusual for some to come out inappropriately. And your job as parents is to provide a boundary, a space for brainstorming solutions and, importantly, not to make too big a deal of it.

The three-point plan about finding out what the inconvenient behaviour is communicating, then problem-solving, then brainstorming, is not the only way to deal with it. Families find their own ways through these milestones, and their own ways to repair a rupture. Here is Sophia's story.

When I came home from work, I smelled smoke. I went into the living room and Camila, my daughter, aged sixteen, was there with her friend. I had never been particularly keen on this friend of hers because there always seemed to be some drama going on to do with her.

So, I turned to the friend and said, 'Have you been smoking?' My daughter said quietly, 'No, Mum, we both have,' but I didn't want to hear that, and I carried on addressing my lecture to her friend, telling her that I didn't appreciate her smoking in my house. My usually nicely behaved daughter went ballistic. She started shouting at me, 'No, Mum, it was me! Stop picking on her! Why don't you ever listen?'

When her friend left, she ran out of steam. I felt shocked because this outburst was unusual for her. I said, 'I'm disappointed that you talked to me like that. I don't want you around right now. Go upstairs.' When my husband, Adam, came in I told him what had happened. He reminded me that we both used to smoke, and that I'd started at her age. And that our daughter was just pointing out that she was fed up of being seen like an angel and her friend being seen like the devil. He also said I'd made up my mind too quickly about her friend.

Adam got me to see it from Camila's point of view. And when I also remembered what the teenage brain is like, I began to calm down.

As Adam and I were talking, I was rolling out ready-made pastry to put on the top of a leftovers pie. So I cut out the letters for 'SMOKING KILLS' and put them on the top of the pie. It was a peace offering to my daughter. When she came down for dinner, she was sheepish. But when she saw the pie she laughed, then we all laughed, and the tension dissipated.

Camila took a picture and put it on Facebook and told the story of being caught smoking, having a screaming match with me – and our newly named 'pie of peace'. One of her friends commented that I should have made a pie of cigarette ends and made her eat it – but not even I would go that far!

Remember this when you're going through a rough time with your teenager: if you usually manage to listen and see the situation from their point of view as well as your own, in the not-too-distant future you'll be able to look back on scenarios like this and laugh together. In other words, you will repair the rupture, especially if you make the first move. Which might be making a pie of peace or, more likely, using words.

It is also important to remember not to deny what their experience of you is. As adults, we do not tend to evolve and develop as quickly as our children, and the picture we may have of our teen may have been accurate six months ago but is not up to date today. So six months ago they may have welcomed your help with their homework, but these days they experience it as annoying interference. Remember not to get defensive when you are told by them that you are annoying or just plain wrong. Although, if your limit is being approached, it may be appropriate to help them find a way of expressing their complaint about you in a fashion in which it would be easier for you to hear. All this becomes easier the more you and your family express your experiences, feelings and boundary settings with self-defining I-statements and not defining-the-other you-statements.

A teenager may temporarily lose some of their charm while they are forging their own identity apart from the family, developing new identity markers to help them form and fit into new tribes. You have not lost your beloved child. Once they feel secure in their new groups of friends in secondary school and then university, their need to feel separate from you will diminish and their better traits will resurface. The teenage brain can have moments as powerful as that of an untamed wild animal. And although it may feel difficult for you as a parent to be empathetic with this at times, keep trying. And be optimistic: their frontal lobes will catch up.

A teenager – and indeed people in their early twenties – might act out the insecurity they feel because they don't yet know their place in life. Insecurity is a type of fear and sometimes, when we feel fearful, our instinct is to attack. Opportunities in some areas for young people can be scarce, while finding a role and forging an identity is a challenge in itself. Remember: we are at our worst just before we have conquered the next hurdle in our life. Young adults need understanding and support to find their way and often the only way they know how to articulate this is by acting out their frustration. This is often inconvenient for those around them and for society in general. Never write someone off as 'bad'. Instead, help them get the help they need. Remember: helping someone is facilitating them to help themselves. When we rescue someone by doing for them what they are capable of themselves, we disempower them and possibly make them feel worse. This means, for example, that we might be alongside them as a wall for them to bounce their ideas off when they are choosing their university, but the choice of what and where they study can usually be left to them. We can remind them that most courses have open days, but the task of looking that up and book-ing a place is probably best left up to them. We can share what we know, but that might not go as far as telling them what to do.

When a teenager acts antisocially, in a way that we had no idea our angel was capable of, what we tend to do as parents is say, 'They've got in with a bad lot.' Every parent of each child in that group may be saying the same thing. For the other parents, your child is the bad one of a bad lot. What is usually happening here is very human, and we all do it; rather than admit our child is as responsible for whatever happened as anyone else's, we blame other people for what happens and see ourselves as inno-cent victims. It's not that anyone is a 'bad lot' so much as that peer pressure is irresistible. Think about what you got up to because of peer pressure when you were a teenager.

Children and teenagers experiment, and that's normal, but of course it doesn't follow that you should find their experiments acceptable. You can share how you feel with them: 'I felt furious when . . .', 'I feel scared when you . . .', 'I am upset that you . . .' But don't waste an opportunity to share more positive feelings as well. 'I felt proud when you . . .', 'I was impressed by you when . . .', 'I'm bursting with love for you when you . . .', and so on.

If you don't dismiss your child's feelings as silly, if you can listen without judging, if you validate their experience of themselves, you are more likely to keep the lines of communication open and they are more likely to continue to confide in you as you both get older. This makes boundary setting – of their boundaries and yours – easier and more natural to maintain.

If there has been a rupture between you, I recommend honesty with yourself about your part in that rupture. If you do not know what it is, I recommend asking them (and not defensively) what needs to be done to mend the rift. Or ask what you could do to make it easier for you and your child to talk more easily. It helps if you remember that older adults do not have the monopoly on being right.

It also helps to remember the simple rule of thumb: define yourself and your feelings, not your child. So, it is 'I'm not ready for you to be going to pubs yet' rather than 'You're too young to go to pubs.'

A client, Liv, was telling me about her relationship with her adolescent son, Matt, sixteen.

> The more time we spend together – doing things together, hanging out together – the easier it is to ask him to do things, like take the sheets off the beds, or empty the dishwasher. When I say, 'Can you do this?' he says, 'Yeah, sure.' But when I'm busy with my own stuff or busier at work so I'm more in my own separate world, when I ask the same thing – 'Can you do this?' – he is much more likely to say, 'No,' or even, 'No, why should I?' In the past, we've got locked into cycles of arguing. But then I'd get less busy at work, more available to just

watch telly together or grab a pizza, and our lives would again become more about cooperation.

I only made this discovery after about ten years of parenting. I said to my husband, 'You can't just live your separate life and then barge into Matt's life and say, "I want you to do this."' It would be a bit like a stranger walking into your house and telling you what to do. The more there is a connection between all of us, the easier it is to work through any problem and negotiate so we each get what we need.

Liv's experience reminds me that it's important to spend time with our children whatever their age, and to listen to them, not only to be with them when we are all staring at separate screens, or living mostly separate lives and merely sharing a space. We need to make sure we connect with them as well as live with them.

When the lines of communication are open, the more complicated, nuanced conversations you need to have about sex, drugs, bullying, friendships, pornography and the online world are easier to have. You can learn how these things are seen by your child and the younger generation and you can each share your feelings and knowledge about them and each change in the process. If you are not willing at all to be impacted upon by the opinions and feelings of your child, they will be less likely to allow your influence and your wise counsel.

If you try to remember what you were like as a teenager, it may help you to find more common ground with your child, although examining your teenage years may give you an unpleasant awakening, as in the quote below.

'In the hope of understanding Bron better, I read the diaries I kept at his age. I was appalled at the vulgarity and the priggishness.'

– Evelyn Waugh, Diary, 1956

Exercise: Maxims for behaviour
- Define yourself rather than defining your child.
- Don't pretend your decisions are grounded in facts when, in fact, they are grounded in your own feelings and preferences.
- Remember you are both on the same side.
- Collaborate and brainstorm rather than dictate.
- A lack of authenticity causes a rupture and you will be able to repair it by becoming authentic.
- And remember: children behave as they are done to.

Exercise: Older teenager as lodger

If you are having difficulties in knowing what boundaries are reasonable for you to ask for with your older teen, imagine they are a lodger who has come to share your home. You would still have house rules, but you would put them in place by defining yourself and not them. For example:

- 'I would like it if you kept your bags in your own room and not the hallway.'
- 'I want you in by twelve because I do not sleep well if I am half expecting to be woken up by you coming in late.'
- 'I am not comfortable with old food plates being kept in the room and cannot allow it.'
- 'You can use the washing machine at any time.'

If you are imagining your nearly-adult child as your lodger, it helps to give them some of the respectful distance they may be craving.

Something for parents to remember: in order to help our children pick up the four cornerstones of appropriate behaviour, we need to keep putting them into practice ourselves. We need to tolerate frustration, be flexible, have problem-solving skills and be able to see things from another's point of view.

And finally: when we're all grown up

Having a child to me feels a bit like this: one minute you are making very slow progress down the road because your toddler's little legs can only take tiny steps. Then for a short while you will be going along at the same pace, and then they will overtake you and you'll have to run to catch up. That last bit – that's the longest bit. That's the bit that all this investment of time, care, consideration, respect and love has been about. That's when they reap the benefits of having a secure attachment style, curiosity about the world and an ability to know what they feel, so that they can work out what they want and need in life and you have the benefits of watching them go for it.

You will have provided them with a secure base, emotionally as well as practically, so if they do get lost along the way – and who doesn't from time to time? – they will have a safe dock to return to that will provide succour and comfort. Even if you are no longer there to come back to, because we are but mortal, they will find that secure base within themselves that was built up in relationship with you and that will help them get back on course.

It means a lot to adult children when their parents take an interest, non-intrusively, in their lives. You always were a mirror for your child. How they see and feel about themselves will always, to some extent, be influenced by how you respond to them, how you delight in them, how you greet them and relate to them. This doesn't suddenly stop when they get to be of voting age, or when they have their own children, or when they retire – it continues. When a hundred-year-old mother beams in delight and shares her pride in her child with them, even though that child may be seventy-five themselves, it is not meaningless; it has affect, it matters. Our pride in our adult children means a lot to them, quite often more than the admiration and praise of others. Don't take part of the credit for their triumphs (unless they give it to you) because it does not help them, but don't side-step from your part in any of their setbacks either.

It is never too late to attempt to repair a rupture, although it helps if you are both still alive. The way to do it, as it ever was, is to look for the feelings behind your behaviour and their behaviour and to try to understand those feelings. If, for example, you feel affronted because your adult offspring warns you off your new lover as not being good for you, don't assume they are trying to keep you all to themselves or are being rude but rather that they are concerned for you and that they love you, and talk back to their concerned part and not the part you want to punish for telling you what might be an inconvenient truth. The roles of parent and child may swap over, and you can find yourself parented by your child.

It can help our adult children to know how we may have made mistakes that led to them making poor decisions. And I'm sorry if this seems unfair. 'It's not fair' was my first idea for a title for this book, because the grown-ups have to invest a lot of their time in their children and, however considerate we are with it, parenting comes with no guarantees.

One way parents can slip up once they imagine their duties are largely over is that they can feel competitive towards their child, or one of their children, and when that child tells them of an achievement they feel they have to top it or come back with a triumph of their own. For example, here's Julie's experience.

> I told my mum how well her grandson was doing at school and, instead of being happy for us, she just came back with how clever my sister had been at school, which felt hurtful, and it wasn't even true. It was as though she was trying to trump me. I asked her why she was being competitive and she just got flustered and changed the subject.

The grandmother here may have just been reminded of her pride in her children by hearing her daughter's pride about her son, but it certainly came out all wrong. When our children are adults, it is just as important as it always was not to fear being in the wrong, not to get flustered when we make a mistake but instead to repair the rupture. It can help to stay aware of our past habits of rivalry such as fact tennis, or winning and losing, because we might slip up and forget about our self-awareness when we think our job is done and then these unhelpful ways of relating can rear their heads again. Even though everyone is now all grown up, because of their past dependence and the child–parent bond, parents may still have a major influence on how their adult children feel about themselves and their lives. We need to keep this in mind so that we do not unknowingly knock them back, as in the above example, or feel so merged with them that we unthinkingly let our inner critic loose on them.

Our bonds with our children can be some of the most important and formative relationships of our lives, and we need to continue to look after these relationships by continuing to respect them when they are adults, as well as loving them.

And just as I recommended looking back to our own childhoods to notice how they are influencing our children's childhoods, it's good to see how our own parents are to us now that we are adults, and what we will do the same as them and what we will want to do differently when our own children are grown up.

Further down the line, if we are lucky enough to live long, we may have to let our children make decisions for us in the final stages of this lifelong relationship. If we have learned to trust them, this will be easier on us, and on them. Having a child means that you will have to be the parent when they are a child, then you will be adults together and, finally, you may become the child to their adult. If we can be flexible and fluid about these roles, it can make it easier on everyone.

Epilogue

Dressing them, feeding them, washing them and putting them to bed . . .

Let's go back to the introduction and the comedian's joke of the four things you need to do with children: 'get them dressed, feed them, wash them and put them to bed'. Doing this – being a parent – might not be the picnic you envisaged, but I hope it will be easier when you do the following things:

- You put aside any blocks from your own childhood that inhibit your warmth and acceptance, physical touch, physical presence and understanding.
- You create a safe, harmonious home environment where differences can be worked through safely.
- You accept your child needs play with people of all ages, soothing experiences and a lot of your attention and time.
- You can see situations from your child's point of view as well as your own.
- You can help your child's need to find ways to express how they really feel (rather than how you wish they felt), and you can validate and attempt to understand their feelings (and your own).
- You don't rush in to rescue them but help them find their own solutions by allowing them to brainstorm to come up with answers to their problems and not being in a rush to tell them what to do.
- You put down your boundaries by defining yourself rather than telling them what they are like.

- You accept that you will make mistakes. You can be non-defensive about those mistakes and repair the situation by owning the mistake and making any necessary change.
- You put aside old dynamics like winning and losing and instead take up cooperation and collaboration.

In other words, you treasure your relationship with your child because you know a safe, loving, authentic, accepting relationship with you is what they need above all else.

Remember: when there is a problem, do not just concentrate on the child and do not think the problem just lies with them. Look at your relationship and what's happening between you. That's where you'll find your answer.

These general rules apply whatever your age and whatever the age of your child.

What is amazing is that, despite all the mistakes we make, all the love we hold back from giving, all the anger we dump on our child, all the times we rush them and all the times we hide from them or make ourselves unavailable to them or don't trust them when we should, or refuse to see things from their standpoint, or overidentify and merge with them and don't allow them to separate, or ask too much of them, we are still bonded to them and they to us.

It's reassuring that we can make that bond better and stronger by being honest and brave enough to repair any ruptures, by being forgiving of ourselves and realizing that we all do our best. We can help and encourage them to aim for what they wish and hope and dream about. And we can believe in them. And I believe in you.

My Response to Feedback About the Book

The best part about writing this book has been talking about it up and down the country, at book shops, festivals, village halls and theatres. And the best part about talking about the book has been the questions from parents. It moves me when I hear from parents who want to get things right with and for their children.

The other day at an event, a mum asked this: 'I am working hard to have the best relationship I can with my two children, but my wider family criticize me for the way I am with my kids. It makes me uncomfortable. What can I do?' My long answer was: 'Great, you are prioritizing your relationship with your children. That is your responsibility, your job, the most important thing right now. You can use your assertiveness skills to show you've heard your relations by thanking them for letting you know what they think, but you *do not have to take up their suggestions.*' My shorter answer was: 'It sounds as if you come from a judgy family, you could even tell them where to go.' (In the live version, I used a stronger word.)

What this flagged up for me, yet again, is that we are all operating in the imperfect environment that is real life. It's a great example of how we're all muddling along, doing the best we can. And that's what makes it so gratifying to hear about the positive effects that *The Book You Wish Your Parents Had Read* has had on real-life family relationships.

Many parents have been telling me how they've been verbalizing their kids' feelings, even when they felt so uncomfortable with their child being furious or inconsolable. They saw that it's true that when a child is seen and understood, that child really doesn't have to shout as loud.

One mum told me about three-year-old Ella having a mega, red-faced screaming tantrum. Such an incident would usually have sent Mum into her own personal meltdown too. But after taking on board the section on tantrums, she got down to the child's level and said, 'You are very angry, aren't you? You poor thing.' She said Ella looked surprised and, a minute later, stopped crying. And soon after that, Ella said, 'I'm sorry I was angry, Mum.' The mum said it was all she could do not to burst into tears of joy!

Dan, father to eleven-year-old Luke, is fairly typical. He told me he used to get into terrible battles with his son about just about everything. They loved each other, but they fought. Then he read the book and decided to not be the one who made all the decisions, had all the answers and was always in charge but instead be someone who was curious about what his son was feeling and how he experienced the world differently to Dan. His unexpected reward was that Luke has stopped having to be right too.

Since publishing this book, I must have communicated with hundreds of parents – both in person and via social media messages. And it seems the biggest hurdle parents must climb is letting go of the notion that their children should be happy all the time. I get asked things like: 'What can I do? My little boy is so sad when his dad has to go away for work,' and 'What should I say? Our neighbours are moving and my daughter is distraught that she'll be losing her playmates.'

And I have to keep saying that, paradoxically, when we just want the kids to be happy, we put unnecessary and added pressure on them. We need to support and be alongside our children in all their feelings. It's a hard one to take on board because our natural inclination is to fix what's hurting. Yet the best fix of all is to keep our kids company in whatever they are going through. Then, when they are anything other than happy, they don't feel they're failing.

What really matters is for us to nurture good relationships in which our children feel seen, valued and understood. For this paperback edition, I've written this new chapter to say a bit more about creating good parent–child relationships, and added some information about how to encourage sibling relationships to become supportive rather than combative. I hope that this can help many more families to reconnect, to repair their ruptures and to form stronger bonds.

The human mirror

A mum, SL, wrote on social media about having read *The Book You Wish Your Parents Had Read*, saying, 'My whole way of being a parent has changed.' She said she now tries to see the world from her two small daughters' point of view, to talk to them about how they feel, to label their emotions, to brainstorm their problems. She takes deep breaths when she feels cross, asking herself, 'Is it worth losing my temper over this?'

'The girls have become calmer, more affectionate to each other, as have my husband and myself. I can't thank Philippa enough for making me a better parent. Sadly, she's also made me realize how my own upbringing lacked real attention. Although love was professed and no doubt felt, it just wasn't shown. But I have learned to show it to my girls.'

There was one particular sentiment she wrote about that really struck a chord with me. And it was: 'The best change is in me. Now I look forward to seeing them *all* the time. I miss them when they're at school.'

Can you imagine how good *you'd* feel if someone felt that about you? And if they showed it too? I'm sure when SL sees her children after school they can see the love shining out of their mum's face.

What SL has hit on is another way to help your relationship, called mirroring. We all need people who light up when we come into the room. And we especially need it when we are babies and little children.

British paediatrician and psychoanalyst Donald Winnicott created the concept of mirroring. He said that the infant 'looks at the mother and sees himself'.

What he means is that the expression on his (or her) parent's face, their delight or otherwise in them, will form within them their sense of self. And, over time, they build up a picture of themselves by how they appear through their parent's responses and reactions to them – or the lack of them.

They look at you and feel whether you are delighted with them, or angry, or loving, or fake, or warm, or indifferent, and in turn they can see how they are affecting you. This all goes in their inner bank.

So, if a parent is joyful on seeing their child, is happy to interact with them and shows their delight in being with them, the child will internalize this and come to see themselves as a valued, loved and lovable person.

If a parent consistently acts as a negative mirror, that has the opposite effect. That can mean being absent, either physically or emotionally, or disinterested, or that the parent banishes them when they show their individuality, or doesn't focus on them except to treat them like a chore or something that needs correction, or never looks up from their phone. We all do all of this occasionally, but when parental behaviour like this is the norm, then the child will build up a picture of themselves as unworthy of love or as a 'bad' person.

A lack of any sort of parental mirroring can be even worse, leading to life-long states of mind in which people feel that they do not really count, and this can make them unduly attention-seeking or depressed.

That doesn't mean you should plaster a fake grin on your face. That's giving your child a false mirror. Rather, you love your children but don't take it so much for granted that you forget to show it. Let the love out. And show it first, before you tell them to wipe their feet or do their homework.

Over the years, I have had many psychotherapy clients who told me something along the lines of, 'I don't think I'm a very nice person.'

One client, Angus, said this early on in our work together. I asked him why he thought he wasn't very nice, but he couldn't be more specific. 'I'm just a bad person,' he said.

He came across as intelligent, he spoke with a nuanced vocabulary, he was a professional, was married with a child and the marriage wasn't in trouble – he had all the outward signs of success, but it was hard for him to be more articulate about being 'a bad person'; it was almost as though the idea was planted within him before he had words.

But, he said, he often felt as if his marriage and his job were an act. And that one day he would be 'found out' and his life would disintegrate. Or he'd feel compelled to make it fall apart, like a self-fulfilling prophecy.

Angus lived about a two-hour drive from his parents. He felt he 'had to' go to see them at least four times a year, yet he always dreaded it. He told me his wife had commented that when he was there he was always a bit quieter than his usual self.

I asked him why he visited his parents. He said the guilt if he didn't was worse than having to go. And anyway, if he didn't do his duty by them, it would prove he was a bad person. 'They seemed perpetually disappointed in me when I was growing up. I always felt I had to try to be better. I never succeeded, though.'

'It's not that they are bad people. But I think that their idea is, if they criticize me, it will make me a better person. I think it does come from a place of love. I think they want me to be accepted in the world and think that I might be more successful if I was more this or more that.'

Of course, Angus had no memory of how he was mirrored as a baby. But he did tell me that when he visited with his new baby his parents kept asking him whether she was a 'good' baby. They meant that she didn't cry, slept a lot and didn't demand anything of her parents.

'That's not a "good" baby,' I said, 'that's an invisible baby, a baby that doesn't exist.' Angus went on, 'As soon as my daughter makes any sort of noise, they turn and frown at her. It's as though she isn't supposed to have feelings or needs.'

He realized from this that his parents probably often frowned at him as a baby, and maybe as a child, as if he wasn't supposed to have feelings or needs either. Over his childhood, he told me how he had experienced their criticism – their trying to make him more 'acceptable' – as being unacceptable, full stop.

Now he was aware of that pattern, he became clear on what he did want for his daughter. 'I try to show my daughter love and acceptance,' he said. 'It's not that I say "I love you" to her all the time. It's just that I don't want to pass this unnecessary criticism down to another generation.' 'You want her to know she is good enough just as she is and that you delight in her,' I said. 'And it will show in your face.'

We might keep our love to ourselves, like Angus's parents seemed to have done, in the mistaken belief that if our children feel accepted in every way, they'll become self-satisfied and won't try to improve. In truth, a child will feel motivated to improve if they know you love them exactly as they are. If they don't feel good enough, they're more likely to give up. It might seem paradoxical, but it's the way it works.

Be interested in what they are interested in

Another way to be a positive mirror is to be interested in what your child is interested in, so it becomes part of them. This isn't a technique, rather it's following their interest to see if you can get interested in it too, from Lego to *Star Wars*, to *Minecraft* and

Extinction Rebellion. When our parents care about what we care about, it's a good feeling.

Jane's six-year-old son Axel had a passion for football, although it wasn't her thing. But he was so into it he kept asking her to take him to a match. She bought tickets to see their local team, Watford City. And because he loved it so much, she caught his enthusiasm. Then she became completely swept up in it – and now she knows the names of all the players.

It might be unrealistic to be interested in everything your child is interested in. As a friend of mine says, 'Alf can talk about Dungeons & Dragons for hours. Sometimes I'm not that interested in the differences between orcs and half-orcs.' But even if you can't manage Dungeons & Dragons, there will be some subjects where you can find common ground.

As a teenager, your child might stop wanting you to be interested in their interests, whether it's *Fortnite* or their music. That needs respecting too. As they've probably let you know with their behaviour, a teenager needs some privacy and a separate life to form their own identity. When they're at this age there's a thin line between being interested and intrusive, so you will need to be sensitive to their boundaries or territory. And take both of those seriously, not personally.

Sibling relationships

At the events I speak at I'm asked a lot about siblings. Mirroring comes up here too: it's an important part of your relationship with each of your children. Although we are all very much part of our tribe, each child needs to be seen and attuned to as the individuals they are.

That is one reason the book talks about you in relation to a child, rather than 'the children'. We should try not to think of our children as 'the children' too often.

Of course, sibling relationships are key to harmony in your tribe. Thinking about your own siblings, if you had them, where did your relationship go right or wrong with them? Things that probably didn't help were your parents comparing you, labelling you – for example, 'the one who's good at sports', 'the noisy one'. Or not challenging you when you made comparisons: 'I'm better at maths' or 'She's cleverer than me.' Or when your parents lumped you together rather than respecting your individuality and differences, for example, 'Kids are so tiring.'

Another biggie is if you felt your sibling got more parental resources at your expense. Then, instead of being angry at your parents, you might resent your sibling. As nobody feels like volunteering for resentment, parents often don't challenge this resentment or ask their child to redirect it at themselves. But the more the resentment between siblings builds, the more the long-term functionality of the relationship between them is threatened.

What follows is a story of what life might be like for a stay-at-home parent with a toddler and a newborn, and one way the sibling relationship might begin to develop.

> The kitchen floor is covered in bits of food and sticky with spills. There's washing-up on every surface. Maryam glances around and feels the weight of the mess. Toddler Noah tugs on one hand and, with the other, she supports baby Suki, who is beginning to grizzle, over her shoulder. 'Come and see my tower!' says Noah.
>
> Maryam feels pulled in all directions. The baby wants her, Noah wants her and the housework does too. She also feels very alone, the only adult, in charge of two people who don't give her a moment to herself.
>
> 'Let's see this tower, then,' Maryam says to Noah. It is, of course, the last thing she wants to do, and that shows in her face.

Noah pulls her through to the living room. It looks like a bomb has hit it too. Every toy is out, in bits and spread over the floor.

'Where's the tower?' The baby's grizzling is turning into wailing. 'It gone,' says Noah, who begins to wail too. Maryam sits down and puts Suki to her breast, but the baby is fussing and won't latch on. Noah tries to get on to Maryam's lap too, but can't, so he pushes Suki.

Maryam knows Noah feels displaced but at that moment she forgets, feels furious and pushes him away, saying, 'Don't push your sister.'

Cue: wailing all round. It all feels too much for Maryam. She manages to put Suki in her basket and Noah in his playpen. She shuts herself in the kitchen, sits at the table with her head in her hands while the children's cries reach a crescendo.

Five minutes later, she comes back into the living room. She puts on a cartoon for Noah to distract him while she tries to feed Suki. Noah stops crying and, eventually, Suki goes to sleep.

If you can try to make it so the older child's relationship with their sibling is more associated with good feelings rather than conflicted ones, they will enjoy being with them. And the younger one will then benefit from their older sibling's input into how they form too.

One way of doing this is not to tell the oldest child that they are delighted to have a new brother or sister. But do help that child put into words what they feel about having to share their parents, even if this is not what you would like them to feel.

If you have established reciprocal relational habits with your first-born rather than the 'doer and done to' dynamic, your children are more likely to have this type of relationship too. But it's never too late to do this. It's great to include the older child in the care of the younger. 'What d'you think the baby needs?'

'Can you remember being this little?' 'D'you remember playing peekaboo? Can you teach the baby to play that?'

It's also good to have some one-to-one alone time with each child every day. Even a few minutes is better than none. Remember: continue to see and treat each child as the individual they are.

If Maryam had taken on board the lessons in this book, her morning might have gone a bit more like this:

> 'You want me to see your tower very much, but first I am going to see to Suki's grizzling, because she hasn't learned to wait yet.' Maryam acknowledges what Noah wants and also tells him her minute-to-minute plans and puts down a boundary so she doesn't feel pulled in two directions.
>
> 'No! See my tower first.' Maryam feeds back to Noah what she imagines he's feeling: 'It's so hard for you to share me now Suki has come along. You were used to having me all to yourself. That is very hard.'
>
> Noah isn't getting what he wants . . . but he is being sympathized with in his disappointment, rather than being told off for having wants, so he doesn't need to demonstrate how he feels. Maryam's tone conveys to him that although he hasn't got her to himself, she's still thinking about him.
>
> Maryam begins to feed Suki and keeps talking to Noah. 'You have a tower to show me, and here I am feeding your sister. It must feel very unfair.' As she looks at him, her face is soft and loving because she is feeling sorry for him not having her to himself.
>
> The truth is, Noah hasn't really got a tower to show Maryam. He invented it because he felt so bad he hadn't got his mother all to himself. He remembers being praised for towers. Now, Mum seems to know how he feels. He feels better and goes into the living room to play while Maryam nurses Suki. Maryam enjoys staring at Suki while she feeds and Suki gazes back at her.

Then Noah is back. 'Mum, I can't find my blocks.' 'If we are both very quiet, Suki will go to sleep. Then we can find them together and have some time, just us two.' Maryam feels relaxed, so Suki feels relaxed. And Noah believes her, because he is beginning to recognize that Maryam does what she says she'll do.

Suki's eyes are beginning to close and, after a couple of minutes, she's asleep. Maryam lays her in her basket, goes into the living room and sees that Noah is absorbed with some toy cars. She sits and watches him. As Noah feels she's available, he doesn't have to be loud or do anything else to get her attention.

After a while he smiles at her, and she smiles back. Maryam gets down on the floor and starts to put some of the toys in the toy bins. Noah says, 'You've found my blocks.' 'They were hiding under the train set,' says Maryam. He leaves what he was doing and starts playing with the blocks. Because Noah feels secure that she is interested in him, he becomes absorbed, and Maryam picks up last Sunday's colour supplement from the table and manages to read half an article uninterrupted.

Suki starts to cry. 'Suki wants you,' says Noah. 'Go to see what she wants,' says Maryam, giving Noah responsibility. He goes into the kitchen and peers at his sister, who stops crying. 'She wanted you,' Maryam says. Now Noah feels valued by his sister.

The main difference between the two scenarios is that in the second one Maryam acts as a positive mirror for Noah and Suki. She allows her love and positive feelings for the other person to show. She tries to anticipate how Noah might feel, and names what she thinks he's feeling, even when it's not a positive emotion. And although it takes longer, she includes Noah in tasks, like checking on Suki. In the second scenario, Maryam also puts down a loving boundary before she reaches her limit; she doesn't come to see Noah's tower at the start of the story because it is too much for her, but neither does she resent being asked.

As children get older than Noah and Suki, the relationship between them will need even more looking after. Here are some things that will help:

Don't heap higher expectations on to the older child. This can breed extra resentment in them towards their younger siblings. Don't, for example, expect the older child to tidy up the toys while the younger one is allowed to sit and watch. The younger one can do what they are capable of. And if they really are a tiny baby, you can talk them through it: 'Look at how Sophia is putting the dolls back in the box. That is exactly where they go.' Because they won't resent you for those expectations, they'll resent their younger sibling.

Watch out for roles. Sometimes in a family, because one child can do, say, gymnastics really well, another thinks that gymnastics has somehow been taken, so they cannot pursue this, even though they may love it. It's not unusual to find a determined and accomplished first-born in a family and a less motivated second- and third-born, with later children assuming a certain talent has somehow been taken by the oldest. Don't get into a habit of comparing the children, even when you're not in front of them, as they will pick up on it. Instead, emphasize the enjoyment of an activity and praise the effort that goes into it. If you glorify the level of accomplishment, it will put off the younger children.

During sibling disputes, slow everything down, finding out the feelings behind each child's behaviour. Then understand and validate how each child is feeling and put that into words for them. Don't get into the habit of declaring who is right and who is wrong, who is bad and who is good.

Once you've established the problem, get them to brainstorm the solution: 'You feel furious when your sister has your bike,' and 'You really resent that your brother has been given a better bike than you by his godfather.' 'The situation is making neither of you happy, and yet our family is richer to the tune of one great bike. What do you think you two could do to make this work? What ideas have you each got?' As they get better at cooperation and compromise, you will have less and less to do with the process.

Family life is never going to be perfect. But just because perfection isn't attainable doesn't mean we should stop being aware of the impact we have on our children and trying to improve it. As a client once said to me, 'Perfection isn't love, but love is perfection.'

So many of us are trying our hardest to be the best and most loving parents we can. Not by pretending the mistakes, muddles and misattunements never happened or aren't happening, but by doing our best to repair them.

Because this is how relationships work: trial and error. We observe and listen to the other person, we examine ourselves and, together, we work out ways we can be together so we can all thrive.

Thank you so much for reading, reflecting and working so hard. By having kind, genuine relationships with your children and each other and providing a safe human environment for them, you are nurturing human beings who are more likely to turn out to be loving, powerful, thoughtful and moral citizens, which is better for all of us.

Further Reading/Listening/Watching

Part One: Your Parenting Legacy

Steven J. Ellman, 'Analytic Trust and Transference: Love, Healing Ruptures and Facilitating Repairs' (Ph.D., pp. 246–63, published online 25 June 2009)

Robert Firestone, *Compassionate Childrearing* (Plenum Publishing/ Insight Books: 1990)

John Holt, *How Children Fail* (Penguin: 1990)

Part Two: Your Child's Environment

Judy Dunn and Richard Layard, *A Good Childhood: Searching for Values in a Competitive Age* (Penguin Books: 2009)

Emily Esfahani Smith, 'Masters of Love. Science Says Lasting Relationships Come down to – You Guessed It – Kindness and Generosity' (https://www.theatlantic.com/health/archive/2014/06/happily-ever-after/372573/)

John M. Gottman, *The Seven Principles for Making Marriage Work* (Prentice Hall and IBD: 1998)

Virginia Satir, *Peoplemaking* (Souvenir Press: 1990)

D. W. Winnicott, *Home is Where We Start From: Essays by a Psychoanalyst* (Penguin: 1990)

Part Three: Feelings

Dr Tom Boyce, *The Orchid and the Dandelion* (Penguin: 2019)

Adele Faber and Elaine Mazlish, *How to Talk so Kids Will Listen and Listen so Kids Will Talk* (Piccadilly Press: 2012)

———, *Siblings without Rivalry* (Piccadilly Press: 2012)

Jerry Hyde, *Play from Your Fucking Heart* (Soul Rocks: 2014; reprint)

Janet Lansbury, 'Five Reasons We Should Stop Distracting Toddlers and What to Do Instead' (http://www.janetlansbury.com/2014/05/5-reasons-we-should-stop-distracting-toddlers-and-what-to-do-instead/)

Adam Phillips, Video on pleasure and frustration (https://www.nytimes.com/video/opinion/100000001128653/adam-phillips.html)

Naomi Stadlen, *What Mothers Do* (Piatkus: 2005)

Donald Winnicott, The 'Good-enough Mother' radio broadcasts (https://blog.oup.com/2016/12/winnicott-radio-broadcasts/)

Part Four: Laying a Foundation

Further information about breast crawl: http://breastcrawl.org/science.shtml

Beatrice Beebe and Frank M. Lachmann, *The Origins of Attachment: Infant Research and Adult Treatment* (Routledge: 2013)

John Bowlby, *A Secure Base* (Routledge: 2005)

Barbara Katz Rothman, *The Tentative Pregnancy: Amniocentesis and the Sexual Politics of Motherhood* (Rivers Oram Press: 1994; 2nd edn)

David F. Lancy, *The Anthropology of Childhood* (Cambridge University Press: 2014; 2nd edn)

Janet Lansbury's blog: JanetLansbury.com

Brigid Moss, *IVF: An Emotional Companion* (Collins: 2011)

Annie Murphy Paul, *Origins: How the Nine Months before Birth Shape the Rest of Our Lives* (Hay House: 2010)

Joan Raphael-Leff, *Parent–Infant Psychodynamics* (Anna Freud Centre: 2002)

———, *Psychological Processes of Childbearing* (Centre for Psychoanalytic Studies: 2002; 2nd rev. edn)

Part Five: Conditions for Good Mental Health

Beatrice Beebe et al., 'The Origins of 12-Month Attachment: A Micro-analysis of 4-Month Mother–Infant Interaction' (https://www.ncbi.nlm.nih.gov/pmc/articles/PMC3763737/)

Ruth Feldman, 'Parent–infant Synchrony and the Construction of Shared Timing; Physiological Precursors, Developmental Outcomes, and Risk Conditions', *Journal of Child Psychology and Psychiatry* (Wiley Online Library: 2007)

———, 'Biological Foundations and Developmental Outcomes' (http://journals.sagepub.com/doi/10.1111/j.1467-8721.2007.00532.x)

Tracy Gillett, 'Simplifying Childhood May Protect against Mental Health Issues' (http://raisedgood.com/extraordinary-things-happen-when-we-simplify-childhood/)

Maya Gratier et al., 'Early Development of Turn-taking in Vocal Interaction between Mothers and Infants' (https://www.ncbi.nlm.nih.gov/pmc/articles/PMC4560030/)

Elma E. Hilbrink, Merideth Gattis and Stephen C. Levinson, 'Early Developmental Changes in the Timing of Turn-taking: A Longitudinal Study of Mother–Infant Interaction' (https://www.ncbi.nlm.nih.gov/pmc/articles/PMC4586330/)

Oliver James, *Love Bombing: Reset Your Child's Emotional Thermostat* (Routledge: 2012)

Janet Lansbury, *Elevating Child Care: A Guide to Respectful Parenting* (CreateSpace Independent Publishing Platform: 2014)

———, *No Bad Kids: Toddler Discipline without Shame* (CreateSpace Independent Publishing Platform: 2014)

W. Middlemiss et al., 'Asynchrony of Mother–Infant Hypothalamic-Pituitary-Adrenal Axis Activity following Extinction of Infant

Crying Responses Induced during the Transition to Sleep' (https://www.ncbi.nlm.nih.gov/pubmed/21945361)

Maria Montessori, *The Absorbent Mind* (BN Publishing: 2009)

S. Myriski et al., 'Digital Disruption? Maternal Mobile Device Use is Related to Infant Social-Emotional Functioning' (https: www.ncbi.nlm.nih.gov/pubmed/28944600)

Darcia F. Narvaez, 'Avoid Stressful Sleep Training and Get the Sleep You Need: You Can Survive the First Year Without Treating Your Baby Like a Rat' (https://www.psychologytoday.com/blog/moral-landscapes/201601/avoid-stressful-sleep-training-and-get-the-sleep-you-need)

——, 'Child Sleep Training's "Best Review of Research": Sleep Studies are Multiply Flawed Plus Miss Examining Child Wellbeing' (https://www.psychologytoday.com/blog/moral-landscapes/201407/child-sleep-training-s-best-review-research)

——, *Neurobiology and the Development of Human Morality* (W. W. Norton & Co.: 2014)

Barry Schwartz, *The Paradox of Choice: Why More is Less* (Harper-Perennial: 2005)

Jack P. Shonkoff and Andrew S. Garner, 'The Lifelong Effects of Early Childhood Adversity and Toxic Stress' (http://pediatrics.aap publications.org/content/early/2011/12/21/peds.2011-2663.short)

Ed Tronick, *The Neurobehavioral and Social-Emotional Development of Infants and Children* (W. W. Norton & Co.: 2007)

Part Six: Behaviour: All Behaviour is Communication

Hannah Ebelthite, 'ADHD: Should We be Medicalising Childhood?' (http://www.telegraph.co.uk/health-fitness/body/adhd-should-we-be-medicalising-childhood/)

Adele Faber and Elaine Mazlish, *How to Talk so Teens Will Listen and Listen so Teens Will Talk* (Piccadilly Press: 2012)

Ross Greene, *The Explosive Child* (Harper Paperbacks: 2014)

Christine Hooper and Margaret Thompson, *Child and Adolescent Mental Health: Theory and Practice* (CRC Press: 2012; 2nd edn)

Janet Lansbury, *Elevating Child Care: A Guide to Respectful Parenting* (CreateSpace Independent Publishing Platform: 2014)

———, *No Bad Kids: Toddler Discipline without Shame* (CreateSpace Independent Publishing Platform: 2014)

Ian Leslie, *Born Liars: Why We Can't Live without Deceit* (Quercus: 2012)

Ruth Schmidt Neven, *Emotional Milestones from Birth to Adulthood: A Psychodynamic Approach* (Jessica Kingsley Publishers Ltd: 1997)

Victoria Talwar and Kang Lee, 'A Punitive Environment Fosters Children's Dishonesty: A Natural Experiment' (https://www.ncbi.nlm.nih.gov/pmc/articles/PMC3218233/)

Acknowledgements

I would like to thank my late parents. Most of the stuff they did was great and the stuff that wasn't was very useful in my career as a psychotherapist and as a writer.

When I was pregnant I knew that I wanted to do some things differently from them and so I turned to a lot of books to educate me. The stand-out ones were: *Compassionate Childrearing* by Robert Firestone; *How to Talk so Kids Will Listen and Listen so Kids Will Talk* by Adele Faber and Elaine Mazlish and *Psychological Processes of Childbearing* by Joan Raphael-Leff. I have found her observations on facilitators and regulators to be invaluable. Firestone's book is about some of the toxic patterns of behaving we inherit and unknowingly pass on, such as our inner critical voice, and Faber and Mazlish write about the wisdom of validating feelings. Their ideas have stayed with me and have been a great help and support in raising my child, and they all influenced this book. I have also been influenced by the work of Donald Winnicott, especially his ideas about when parents hate or resent their children and the work he did to normalize this.

I have read many more since. *Origins: How the Nine Months before Birth Shape the Rest of our Lives* by Annie Murphy Paul was a huge influence on the pregnancy chapter. I recommend that book, along with *The Tentative Pregnancy: Amniocentesis and the Sexual Politics of Motherhood* by Barbara Katz Rothman for expecting parents. But books have not been my only invaluable resource; Janet Lansbury's blog JanetLansbury.com has been a major influence on me and on this book and I highly recommend it when it comes to how to be with toddlers and understanding them. From her I have taken ideas about the undesirability of distracting children away from their feelings, the message about not sitting babies up and the case study about when to help and when not to rescue (Freya). It was also in her blog that I first read how important it is to respect our children as well as loving them. I am grateful to *A Good Childhood: Searching for Values in a Competitive Age* by Judy Dunn and Richard Layard for the research therein about family structure and the implied outcomes for children. *The Anthropology of Childhood* by David F. Lancy is where I got the phrase 'sympathetic magic' and also the concept of child-centric or adult-centric parenting, which built on the ideas I learned from Joan Raphael-Leff. I am indebted to Darcia Narvaez's *Neurobiology and the Development of Human Morality*; her ideas and research have been invaluable to me and especially her collated research around sleep training and its potential to harm. *The Explosive Child* by Ross Greene really helped me define and break down when children behave inconveniently and I found his ideas about collaborative discipline very useful. His is the idea that you need flexibility, problem-solving skills and a tolerance of frustration in order to behave. He also gave me the idea of a letter written from a child's perspective to help parents empathize with their children. These and other books, blogs, podcasts and videos I have relied on are listed in the Further Reading section.

There are also many people I need to thank. I will start with the professionals: I'm indebted to the wisdom of Margaret Connell, the head of my daughter Flo's secondary school, who not only educated my daughter but taught me a lot as well, especially about children and lying. My psychotherapist colleagues to whom I talked when writing this book have my undying gratitude. I have special thanks for my friend Dorothy Charles of Tribal Ground in California. Dorothy helped me with the 'winning versus losing dynamic', and our conversations and her comments on an early draft have been so useful. My buddy, the gestalt body psychotherapist Julianne Appel-Opper of The Living Body in Berlin helped me with many of the concepts in this book, and especially on dialogue, the to and fro of contact and her wonderful attachment-theory metaphor. She read a very early rough draft and gave me invaluable notes. This would have been a poorer book without her. We spent four days in an East German spa brainstorming ideas for the book, and I look forward to another minibreak with her when I am not writing. Nicola Blunden from the University of South Wales was so helpful to bounce ideas off when we stayed together in a cottage on the South Downs in our two-person writing group. Nicky Forsythe, founder and CEO of Talk for Health, London, developed the 'How comfortable are you with your emotions?' exercise, and the 'How to get better at dialogue' exercise was adapted from a 'How to listen' exercise that she teaches at Talk for Health. I owe thanks to the writer Wendy Jones, who, when I was at a low point with the book, facilitated gestalt two-chair work for me, which meant she got me to have a conversation with this book and I became clearer about the direction in which I wanted to take it. Thank you to Louis Weinstock, child and family therapist at Bounce Works, for your encouragement and feedback around technology and around development of a default mood. I am also grateful to the journalist and psychotherapy trainee Suzanne Moore, who said the sentence stressing the importance of 'not only loving children but liking them too'; her phrase stayed with me and influenced the thinking in this book. Thank you to Aaron Balik of Stillpoint, London, who allowed me to use the facilities of Stillpoint Spaces in which to do my edits. You have all been generous with your time, ideas, encouragement and love and I could not have done this without you.

My daughter, Flo, read my first jumbled notes when I wanted to give up and implored me to go on with it. She has also advised me on subsequent drafts. She convinced me it was worth carrying on; if it was not for her, I could not have done this. She has also been very generous in being the only undisguised reappearing case study in the book. I have learned so much about life from Flo. Seeing the world afresh from her eyes has improved me as a writer but, more importantly, as a person. Flo also introduced me to Hannah Jewell, who came to stay with me and was a great writing companion. I am so grateful to my husband, Grayson, for his love, courage and authenticity in the parenting endeavour. It has been wonderful to witness his relationship with Flo and also to have a witness to my relationship with her. And he has had to absorb so much of the pain that I seem to have had to go through in the process of writing this book, and did so uncomplainingly. I am also indebted to many friends who have given me long-standing encouragement. Especial thanks go to: Janet Lee; Yolanda Vazquez and Jonny Phillips; Alba Lily Phillips-Vazquez, Helen Bagnall (who took one photograph of me when I was stuck with the writing of this book, and another when I was more cheerful about it), and she, Diccon Towns and Juliet Russell also introduced me to audiences at Salon London and the Also Festival, which has been so beneficial. All these people have been with me throughout the writing of this book, and I love them all so much. I am also very grateful to those friends I see less regularly but often chat with online. They too have kept my pecker up: thank you to Rose Boyt, who gave me useful feedback on my manuscript, Damian Barr, who invited me to read from a draft of this book to his encouraging audience at his Literary Salon in the glamorous Savoy Ballroom, and Clare Conville, who invited me to the Curious Arts Festival and provided me with a wonderful audience on which to try out some of the ideas in the book. Friends like these have given me courage, and I have needed that courage.

I have talked to many, many parents to find my case studies, and the ones I haven't used have been as valuable as those I have, because they shaped and sharpened my thinking and educated me about what it is like to be a parent, helping me to see that my viewpoint as a parent and as a child is only one of many. Not only have I talked to a lot of parents, but many have written to me, participated in my surveys, talked to me online, contacted me at *Red* magazine, where I have an advice column, and some have been my psychotherapy clients. I am indebted to them all.

I am also grateful to all those children, teenagers and adult children it has been my privilege to come across and learn from, especially my clients, who demonstrated to me time and time again how the patterns of feeling, thinking and responding that are laid down in infancy and childhood can stay around for a long, long time. I thank each and every one of you, as you have been my teachers. I owe especial thanks to the client whose pseudonym in this book is 'Gina' because she not only provided me with case material but also pointed out errors in early drafts and is such a loyal supporter of my work.

I have more teachers to thank too. Professors Maria Gilbert and Diana Smukler ran a psychotherapists' reading and supervision group that met monthly for several years at the beginning of this century. In this group we learned and discussed many concepts, theories and ideas from Relational Psychoanalysis, which I have applied to parenting in this book, but more than providing mere ideas, these two teachers increased my confidence in my ability because of their encouragement of me. I also felt encouraged by my analyst, Professor Andrew Samuels, who showed me that an authority figure does not lose authority when they allow themselves to be vulnerable, unsure and authentic. He also said to me once that there were two sorts of therapists, those who go to workshops and those who run them, and he gave me a much-needed nudge when he said I was in the wrong group. My analysis may have ended years ago, but the positive effects of it go on. I am grateful to all the therapists I have had. Through being in therapy I have learned about the process of being in relationships, and much of that can be applied to any relationship and especially the parent–child relationship.

Thank you to Karolina Sutton, my agent, who took me out to lunch and asked what ideas I had for a book. I told her I could write a book that was about the importance of the relationship you have with your child as a sort of alternative parenting manual and, before I could decide whether I wanted to write it or not, she had set up a meeting with Venetia Butterfield of Penguin Random House. Never has so much lunch been consumed in the making of one book. Venetia took me to lunch on many occasions and we often talked about our experiences of being a parent and I thought we were on the same page. Then she got the first draft and she disliked it. We went through a process of rupture and repair and we collaborated to find a form we both liked. We could have run away from each other, but we did not. I believe relationships that go off course can get back on course again and be stronger and better for it, and how apt that rupture and repair is an important part of this book and that we went through this process ourselves, when Venetia and I were publisher and writer respectively. Thank you for hanging in there, Venetia. I'm also grateful to Aimee Longos, Jack Ramm and Sarah Day for their editorial input.

And lastly, if you are still reading, before I get to the 'and anyone else who knows me', as though I am a contestant signing off from a Radio 2 quiz show, I have to thank my former colleague from *Red* magazine, who expertly edited my advice column for several years, for doing a transformative edit of this book. Brigid Moss asked all the right questions and made me answer them. Brigid Moss, YOU ARE AN UTTER AND COMPLETE BLOODY STAR, a brilliant writer and editor, an awe-inspiring parent, and I love you.

And anyone else who knows me. That might sound trivial, but we all rub off on each other, form each other and sustain each other. For example, 'Show party' mentioned in the section on play is a game devised by one-year-old Esme. About two decades ago, her father, Guy Scantlebury, was building me a new kitchen and sometimes used to turn up for work looking rather tired. 'Show party, 5 a.m.,' he would offer by way of explanation.

Philippa Perry
September 2018

Index

Index

If you enjoyed this, why not also read *Couch Fiction*
by Philippa Perry – out now!

**Ever wondered if therapy was for you? Curious as to what
really happens in a therapist's consultation room? Always
wanted to know what therapists are really thinking?**

From the bestselling author Philippa Perry, this compelling story
of psychotherapy vividly explores what really happens between a
client and therapist throughout a year of therapy sessions.
Sharing fascinating insights into the thoughts of both therapist
and client, this glorious, warm and witty graphic novel shows
the reality of a therapeutic journey as we see their true emotions
unfold and their relationship develop with every session.

Beautifully illustrated by Flo Perry, this illuminating book
offers an insightful and thought-provoking exploration of
therapy, from both sides of the couch.